Persons in Relation

This is the second volume of
Professor John Macmurray's Gifford Lectures
given under the title

THE FORM OF THE PERSONAL

*

Volume 1. The Self as Agent
Volume 2. Persons in Relation

by the same author

*

FREEDOM IN THE MODERN WORLD
REASON AND EMOTION

PERSONS IN RELATION

by

JOHN MACMURRAY
M.C., M.A., LL.D.

FABER AND FABER LIMITED
London

First published in 1961
by Faber and Faber Limited
24 Russell Square, London, W.C.1
First published this edition 1970
Printed in Great Britain by
Latimer Trend & Co. Ltd., Whitstable
All rights reserved

SBN (paper) 571 09404 X
SBN (cloth) 571 05264 9

TO MY WIFE
without whose patient encouragement and help
these volumes would never have seen the light
THIS BOOK IS DEDICATED

Contents

Introductory

This book constitutes the second volume of the Gifford Lectures delivered in the University of Glasgow in 1953 and 1954. The first volume was published, under the title *The Self as Agent*, in 1957. It was concerned to exhibit the primacy of the practical in human experience, and the need to transfer the centre of gravity in philosophy from thought to action. It went on to consider the structural implications of such a change, and the manner in which the forms of reflective activity are derived from and related to action.

The present volume presupposes the conclusions of the first. The reflective activities are solitary, however their results may be published and communicated to others. Consequently, the tradition which conceives man as Thinker must conceive him as a multiplicity of centres of reflection, each inherently unrelated to the others; each standing over against the world which it knows. From this point of view action is strictly inconceivable, and even the reflective activities are restricted to the one which aims at knowledge, the activity of thought. This does not preclude the recognition of other forms of human activity. But if they are practical, they are considered as determinate happenings in the object-world; or else there is postulated, illogically and mysteriously, a point at which a process of thought is prolonged or transformed into a bodily movement. If they are themselves reflective, they are considered in their external manifestations, as they affect an observer. Art, for example, is treated not as a form of reflective activity, but as a set of 'works' to be apprehended and appreciated.

INTRODUCTORY

The effect of transferring the centre of reference to action, and at the same time its sufficient justification, is that man recovers his body and becomes personal. When he is conceived as agent, all his activities, including his reflective activities, fall naturally into place in a functional unity. Even his emotions, instead of disturbances to the placidity of thought, take their place as necessary motives which sustain his activities, including his activity of thinking. For our present purpose, however, the result which concerns us especially is that it ends the solitariness of the 'thinking self', sets man firmly in the world which he knows, and so restores him to his proper existence as a community of persons in relation. It is the purpose of this book to show how the personal relation of persons is constitutive of personal existence; that there can be no man until there are at least two men in communication.

This conclusion has clearly a positive relation to the current linguistic philosophy. Both are concerned to stress the centrality of language for philosophy. To transfer the task of logic from the analysis of thought to the analysis of language is to take a step towards the recognition of the mutuality of the personal and its implication, the primacy of action. But to rest here, to conceive philosophy as *simply* the logical analysis of language, is to fail to see the implications of this step, and to remain stuck in the presuppositions of the philosophical tradition from which it could release us. Language is the major vehicle of human communication. Communication is the sharing of experience. If language is fundamental to human existence, it follows that the human sphere, the field of the personal, cannot be understood through organic categories, in functional or evolutionary terms. It means, in other words, that men are not organisms, that the human world is as distinct from the organic as the organic is from the material, though it is built upon the organic as the organic is upon the material.

The exploration of the structure of this personal world, and the discovery of the categories through which it may be coherently conceived is the task set for philosophy in our time. In a sense this always has been its task, though hitherto it has thought to perform it analogically, by means of mechanical or organic models. Now we can pass beyond these, knowing that they are inadequate and why they are inadequate, and address ourselves to the task directly, using whatever methods the nature of the material demands. To this new enterprise the chapters that follow are intended as a contribution. What I have written can be no more than a preliminary and tentative reconnaissance. I hope that it may indicate a promising direction for advance.

Jordans,   JOHN MACMURRAY
Beaconsfield, Bucks.
July 1960.

CHAPTER ONE

The Field of the Personal

The first volume of this work was preliminary to the consideration of the personal in its full concreteness of being. It was, in my judgment, a necessary preliminary. In that volume we considered the Self as agent, and sketched the outline of a theory of action. But the task to which we addressed ourselves was more radical than such a summary of its content might suggest. For we were led to criticize and to reject the standpoint of our philosophical tradition—the 'I think', and to substitute for it the 'I do'. We had to attempt to think *from the standpoint of action*, whether what we thought about were matters of theory or of practice; of action or of reflection. Our conclusion was not merely that the Self is agent; but that the Self has its being only in its agency, and that its reflective activities are but negative aspects of this agency. The Self as 'the Mind', which is the Self as non-agent, is a nonentity. It follows from this that so long as we maintain, whether consciously or unconsciously, the traditional standpoint, no account of the personal is logically possible. The Self must then be conceived either as a substance or as an organism, while in reality it is a person. Because our final intention was to reflect upon the nature of the personal, it was necessary first to shift the centre of gravity in our reflection from thought to action, and so to achieve an attitude of mind, and a centre of reference from which the Self can appear as an existing being.

This first volume was concerned to criticize the purely theoretical standpoint of our philosophical tradition, and to substitute for it a practical standpoint. But in the course of our study we were driven to recognize another defect of modern philosophy, its egocentricity. These two defects are inherently related. We discovered that the thinking Self—the Self as Subject—is the Agent in self-negation. In reflection we isolate ourselves from dynamic relations with the Other; we withdraw into ourselves, adopting the attitude of spectators, not of participants. We are then out of touch with the world, and for touch we must substitute vision; for a real contact with the Other an imagined contact; and for real activity an activity of imagination. That this self-negation of the Agent is possible, and indeed necessary, there can be no doubt; and to recognize it is to bring to light the form of the personal, as a positive that includes and is constituted by its own negative. But it is possible only within limits. We can contemplate a distant object, but not without remaining in dynamic contact with the ground on which we stand. This contemplation is *per se*, we have seen, the formation of an image. It provides knowledge of the Other only on the assumption of the possibility of contact—that is to say, that the image is rightly referred to an existing other. On occasion this verification by contact proves impossible, and we are convicted of an illusion. The visual experience turns out to have been a mere image which cannot be referred to the Real, or which cannot be *so* referred.

Now if this negative moment in personal experience is used philosophically to determine the nature of the Self, if the Self is determined as the Thinker, the Knower or the Subject, then our actual experience of contemplation is generalized without limit. As a result, the Self must be conceived as *totally* isolated from the Other, not as self-isolated by intention within the reality of its existence as agent; while the Other becomes not a part of the existing reality, abstracted as a particular object by limitation of attention, but the all-inclusive object of thought. The existence of this total object at once becomes problematical, and no verification is at all possible. For all possible objects of knowledge have become equally images, that is to say, representations which demand a reference beyond themselves, and whatever we may refer them to is equally a representation, itself requiring verification. Any distinction between true and false ideas becomes impossible. Indeed, it is impossible to see how the very idea of such a distinction could arise. The Self conceived as 'spectator of all time and all existence' itself becomes a mere idea, since it is excluded from participation in what it contemplates. There is no place for it in the world. And whatever world its vision may be conceived to apprehend consists of its own ideas, as Descartes rightly recognized. It is more illuminating to recognize it frankly as solipsism; and to accept this solipsism for what it is—a *reductio ad absurdum* of the theoretical standpoint. Existence cannot be proved; it is not a predicate. Yet the isolated self—the thinker—must prove existence if he is to apprehend the Other. The given for reflection is always idea— whether it be concept or image, and not less if it be that endproduct of the analysis of sensory experience which is now entitled 'sense-datum'. We know existence by participating in existence. This participation is action. When we expend energy to realize an intention we meet a resistance which both supports and limits us, and know that we exist and that the Other exists, and that our existence depends upon the existence of the Other. Existence then is the primary datum. But this existence is not my own existence as an isolated self. If it were, then the existence of any Other would have to be proved, and it could not be proved. What is given is the existence of a world in which we participate— which sustains and in sustaining limits our wills.

Since then the Self as Subject is the isolated Self, we can transform our earlier conclusion that the Self exists only as Agent. We may say instead that the Self exists only in dynamic relation with the Other. This assertion provides the starting-point of our present argument. The thesis we have to expound and to sustain is that the Self is constituted by its relation to the Other; that it has its being in its relationship; and that this relationship is necessarily personal. Our main effort, therefore, must be directed towards determining the formal characters of personal relationship.

THE FIELD OF THE PERSONAL

It may be useful before going further to consider shortly the terminology which we shall employ. If we change our point of view in philosophy, we are inevitably committed to a change in the meaning of the structural terms we use; for we are then looking at the same things from a new perspective, not at different things from the same perspective. In such a case it is a mistake to seek for new terms. The wiser way is to use, for the most part, the old terms, and allow them gradually to modify their meaning through their use in the new context. If the change of standpoint is justified the new meaning will not be simply a different one, but an ampler and richer meaning; more adequate to the concreteness of living experience. The need for a precisely technical language in science arises because we are dealing with abstract isolates; and our terms must not refer beyond the limits of our abstraction. In philosophy, as in history and in theology, the opposite is the case; in these it is the incompleteness of the abstract which we must avoid, and should not suggest. The effective medium of philosophical language is ordinary speech at its richest, used with precision. We should not forget that a measured precision in the use of language is not peculiar to the scientist. It is also a primary necessity for the poet. Philosophical precision differs from both, since it is determined by its own purposes; but in this, as in other matters, the philosopher's stands closer to the poet's than to the scientist's.

There are, however, certain structural terms in traditional philosophical usage which we should do well to avoid, at least for the present,[1] because they are the product of the inadequate standpoint which we are concerned to abolish. I have in mind, in particular, such terms as 'the Mind', 'the Will', and, above all, 'the Self'. These terms are systematically indeterminate. The necessity for their employment, and the indeterminacy of their reference, derive from the adoption of a purely theoretical standpoint. 'The Self' is a term whose function is to represent

[1] The terms referred to have been used occasionally, for simplicity of statement, in later chapters; but only where no doubt as to their proper reference can reasonably arise.

the subject as object of thought. 'The Mind' and 'the Will' represent the dualist analysis of 'the Self' in its irreconcilable aspects of Thinker and Agent. The indeterminacy of meaning arises from the non-existence of the Subject, in the sense we have already discussed. Its indeterminacy is in effect a concealed contradiction. It is at once a singular and a general term. As singular, it is the unitary centre of all possible experience—what Kant called the Transcendental Unity of Apperception. It is then hypothetical, formal and ideal. It is *hypothetical* as the subjective correlate of our hypothetical knowledge which should be infinitely comprehensive and absolutely coherent—the knower for a completed system of knowledge. It is *formal*, since any assertion anyone makes claims to be true, and has, therefore, the form of an element in such a system. It is *ideal*, since it is what any individual strives to be when he seeks to know the truth. At the same time it is a general term, formed on the analogy of terms like 'the mosquito', 'the pig', 'the lion' or, more appropriately, 'the unicorn'. For you and I and all other individual subjects are subsumed under it, and it refers to any and all of us indifferently. If I read the reflexives 'myself' and 'yourself' as 'my *Self*' and 'your *Self*', then 'Self' becomes the name of something we all possess in common; and can be employed as a generic term to include all beings who, like us, are capable of thought. They are all Selves; and 'the Self' can function as a class concept.

This combination of singularity—as the 'I', with generality—as 'all thinking beings' is possible only if we postulate the *identity* of all the particulars denoted by the term. 'The Self' then is identical in all thinking beings; or to put it otherwise, we are identical in so far as we are rational; and if we think logically we think the same thing in the same connection; if we act rationally, we all do the same thing in the same circumstances. The function of this logical sleight of hand is to conceal the essential differences between individual people; and particularly the formal distinction between 'I' and 'You'. These differences become accidental to our real nature, empirical only, merely psychological. We escape into a logical heaven where error and evil cease to trouble us, where the clash of our mutual contradictions is stilled and the struggle of our antagonistic purposes resolved. With a good conscience we can then consider the world as the unique object known by 'the Self'—though neither you nor I would claim to possess such knowledge; or we can define the truth as that which satisfies 'the Mind', though you and I are by no means always satisfied by the truth that we discover, as when we come to know that someone we trusted as a friend has been maligning us behind our backs.

'The Self', then, and its aspects 'the Mind' and 'the Will' are metaphysical fictions. There are no such entities. They are not, however, gratuitous fictions. They are necessary postulates for any philosophy which proceeds on the assumption, consciously or unconsciously, that we 'can know independently of action; that we can determine truth within the limits of a systematic effort of thought. The formal reason for this necessity is as follows.

The act of thinking is constituted by a purely theoretical intention. It involves a withdrawal from action, and so from all positive, practical relations with the Other. When we think, we shut ourselves within the circle of our own ideas and establish, as it were, a methodological solipsism. We behave as though we were 'pure subjects', observers only, unimplicated in the dynamic relatedness of real existence. Our activity, we assume, makes no difference to the things we think about, but only to our ideas of them, upon which alone we are operative.

There can be no objection to this procedure so long as it remains within the agency of the thinker as its negative aspect. For we recognize that the thinking and its results have a meaning through their reference to our direct commerce with reality in action, in which their truth or falsity can be checked. But when, for philosophical purposes, we adopt a theoretical standpoint, and so define our own being as that of a thinker or subject, then, whether we are aware of it or not, we transform this methodological solipsism into an existential one. We *exist* as thinkers. We are imprisoned in an 'egocentric predicament', and there is no way out. We are committed to explaining knowledge without reference to action.

Philosophers have never, of course, accepted the implications of this position completely. If they did, a total scepticism would be the only possible conclusion. For the reference from theoretical to practical experience provides the only legitimate basis for a distinction between truth and falsity, and it is this reference which has been ruled out. If I am isolated within the circle of my ideas, then they are what they are; or, rather, they are as I think them. If they are to be true or false, it must be by reference to something beyond them, to something which is not ideal but real. What is clearly necessary to the possibility of knowledge is accepted, therefore, in philosophical practice, even if it seems incompatible with the fundamental assumption. Philosophers discuss with one another how any of them can know that the others exist, and find no satisfactory solution. We are so used to this that we no longer notice how comical it is.

This is not the place to consider the various ways in which escapes from this dilemma of the egocentric predicament have been engineered. But there is one implication of the distinction between 'true' and 'false' which is pertinent to our immediate interest. Thinking, like other characteristic activities, is problematic. Whenever we think, we run the danger of falling into error. Part of the meaning of the distinction between truth and falsity lies in a reference to other thinkers. To claim that what I think is true is to require its acceptance by all other subjects. If another disagrees with me, either he is wrong or I am wrong or we are both wrong. In other words, if we all think the truth we all think the same thing, so that it is a matter of indifference, from the theoretical point of view, which particular thinker does the thinking. Consequently, provided we are all thinking the truth, we can treat the particularity of the thinker as a negligible constant.

But can we, even from a purely theoretical standpoint, leave error out of account? We not merely can, but we must. For we are withdrawn from contact with other persons, and cannot discover whether they disagree with us. We cannot be challenged and we must rely on the process of our own thinking. After all, to think is to draw *correct* conclusions. If we fall into error, it must be because we failed to think, not because we thought wrongly. Strictly speaking, so far as we really do think, the possibility of error is excluded. We should remember, also, that to withdraw into the solipsism of reflection does not merely mean to withdraw from physical contact with the Other. Action is not mere movement; and indeed the cessation of movement is not a necessity for thought. What is excluded are those aspects of our personal existence which are directly concerned with action —personal interests, motives, desires, emotions and the rest. And it is these which provide the prejudices and bias that interfere with the proper movement of disinterested thought.

If, then, we start with the solitary individual, self-isolated in reflection, and consider him existing as a thinker, we do exclude the normal sources of error, and his existence becomes an ideal existence. We must recognize the existence of other people, of course, in order to give meaning to the distinction between true and false. But we must exclude *their* concrete, practical existence also, and conceive them, too, as unimplicated observers, as thinkers like ourselves. So, we all rise above the sources of error, which lie in the limitations of a spatio-temporal existence and the practical necessities which it imposes; above bias and prejudice; above the particularities of circumstance and experience which account for our differences from one another. So, we all enter a logical heaven, where there is nothing to sully the pure exercise of reason, and to think is to think the truth. This is the world of 'the Mind', in which 'the Self' has its ideal habitation. For here it is always possible to refer indeterminately to whoever the thinker may be. It is no longer I who think this and you who think that. 'The Mind' thinks, and what it thinks is true because 'the Mind' thinks it.

If the theoretical standpoint of the philosophical tradition is to be maintained, it is not merely possible but also necessary to talk in this fashion. For the problem is to recognize the multiplicity of existing individuals, while safeguarding the isolation of each as a thinker or subject. This can only be done by *identifying* each individual, *qua* thinker or *qua* rational being, with all the others. In this way it is possible to maintain a distinction without a difference. There is a multiplicity of individual thinkers. Each is 'I', an Ego, a Self. But their distinctness is purely numerical; qualitatively they are identical. There are many 'I's'; but there is no 'You', for that would break the isolation and demand an essential difference. Consequently, there is effectively only one thinker—*the* I, *the* Ego, *the* Self, and the many selves are all individuations of the same Self.

The concept of 'the Will' is generated analogously. But here there is a special difficulty to be overcome. The Will is the Self in action. But the concept of the Self involves, as we have seen, the withdrawal from action. It is possible, from the theoretical standpoint, to say that the Mind thinks. It is doubtful whether we can say that the Will acts. There is talk of 'acts of Will', but these are not physical actions, whatever they may be. They seem to refer rather to decisions to act. They seem to come between the thought that 'x' is the right thing to do—which is mental— and the doing of 'x'—which is physical—in order to bridge the gap between them. This it cannot do. For if it is mental, it can no more cause a bodily movement than a thought; and if it can cause a movement of the body, the gap between the act of Will and the Mind is itself unbridged. This is the reason, no doubt, why some have maintained that we are free to will, though all our acts are determined.

This however is hardly our concern at the moment. We are discussing the traditional use of the terms, 'the Mind', 'the Will', 'the Self', and the ground of its necessity. Since the conception of persons as subjects or thinkers is based upon a withdrawal from action, we might expect that it will run into difficulties when practical issues are in question. Our conclusion on the main point is this. The necessity for these terms lies in the egocentricity of the traditional philosophical outlook, and this in turn is a necessary consequence of postulating the primacy of thought.

But we have already disposed of this necessity by asserting the primacy of action; and we no longer need to use these abstract terms. In the first volume of this work we had a reason for retaining them. We had two fundamental criticisms to make of the modern philosophical tradition; first, that it was purely theoretical and, second, that it was egocentric. By using the term 'the Self' and discussing the Self as agent we were able to isolate the former issue and to consider its major consequences without involving ourselves, at the same time, in the effort to overcome the egocentricity which is inseparable from the theoretical standpoint. This separation of two issues which are essentially interconnected seemed desirable from a methodological point of view. In talking of the Self as agent we accepted the traditional abstraction from existence, and initiated a discussion of the *concept* of action. Now we have to take the practical standpoint for granted, and consider the Agent, not as an abstract concept, but in its concrete actuality as existent. The appropriate term here is the term 'person'. Any 'self'—that is to say, any agent—is an existing being, a person. At this point, therefore, our discussion enters the field of the personal. The theme of the present volume can be stated simply. The idea of an isolated agent is self-contradictory. Any agent is necessarily in relation to the Other. Apart from this essential relation he does not exist. But, further, the Other in this constitutive relation must itself be personal. Persons, therefore, are constituted by their mutual relation to one another. 'I' exist only as one element in the complex 'You and I'. We have to discover how this ultimate fact can be adequately thought, that is to say, symbolized in reflection.

The field of our enquiry, then, is the field of the personal, and we have to survey it from the standpoint of action, which is the distinguishing characteristic of the personal. By 'The Field of the Personal' we mean to denote the whole manifold of entities, activities and relations to which the term 'personal' is applicable. But this term itself requires some preliminary consideration, although its full definition can only emerge later, and indeed is in one sense the purpose of our enquiry.

In the first place, I have used the term 'the personal' where it might have seemed more natural to employ the word 'personality'. This is partly because we need a word which is more inclusive and wider in denotation than 'personality' could reasonably be made. But more important is the fact that the term has been diverted from its natural meaning. We should expect it to refer to that quality or set of characteristics in virtue of which a person is a person; a property therefore which all persons share, and which distinguishes a person from all beings which are not personal. In fact, it has been specialized to mean the quality or set of characteristics which distinguishes one person from another. This would more properly be referred to as 'personal individuality'. It is hardly possible to use the term 'personality' now without suggesting the specialized meaning, and so stressing the element of difference between persons instead of what they have in common. It will be advisable, therefore, to avoid the use of this term as much as possible.

'Personal'

This specialization of 'personality' is not, however, simply a historical accident, and the reason for it is instructive. We have seen that if the individual is defined in terms of his negative aspect as a 'thinker' or subject, the generalization which refers this definition to all individuals is achieved through an identification and appears as 'the Self'. As 'selves' all persons are identical, and formally there is only one subject—the subject of all possible experience. This point of view necessitates a dualism; for all individuals must also appear as objects for the subject. Consequently, if we appear at the subjective pole of this dualism in our logical aspect as knowers, we must also appear at the opposite pole as objects of knowledge, and therefore as discriminable elements in '*the* Object' which corresponds to '*the* Self', that is to say, in the world. The 'rational self' must have as its correlate and complement an 'empirical self', or rather a multiplicity of 'empirical selves'. If, then, in our rationality we are simply identical, in our 'personality', which is our empirical self-hood, we are simply different. As subjects we are all 'I'; as personalities, in our empirical existence, there is only one individual 'I'—myself: all other persons are not 'I' but 'You'. Thus to be a 'self' in the empirical sense is to be I and not you; and the concept of 'personality' carries an essential reference to the differentiation of persons, and to the 'otherness' of each personal individual.

We should notice, in passing, that this specialization of the term 'personality' involves a corresponding specialization of the term 'rationality'. Reason is traditionally the *differentia* of the human. If the personal individual is essentially the thinker, then rationality must refer to the logical faculty, and to this faculty in contrast with the empirical capacities which belong to our practical nature, and even to the empirical processes which provide data for a psychological account of thinking. Rationality becomes the capacity to draw correct conclusions from premises; and we postulate that as rational beings this capacity belongs to all of us and is identical in all. This, I say, is a specialization of the term rationality. But to say this is to say too little. For if we use the term in this sense, while at the same time we use it to denote the differentia of the human—that which distinguishes us from the brutes—we are in error. The human *differentia* we have decided is not the capacity to think, but the capacity to act. If, then, we continue to use the term 'rationality' in the specialized theoretical reference we must surrender its use to denote the essential characteristic of the personal. If, on the other hand, we prefer to retain its use as defining the human or personal field as distinct from the non-human, we must give up the specialized reference to logical thought. Reason becomes, then, the capacity to act, and only in a secondary and derivative sense the capacity to think, that is to say, to pursue a merely theoretical intention. It seems to me that there is good reason for choosing this latter course, since choose we must, or abandon the term 'reason' and its derivatives altogether. For the use of reason to denote the *differentia* of man is the more fundamental and the more stable.

The empirical determination of the *differentia* is naturally derivative and variable in principle; and it has in fact varied considerably during the history of philosophy. If it has tended on the whole to have a predominantly theoretical reference, this is because Plato and Aristotle determined the tradition in this direction at the start by their conviction that the good life for man is the 'theoretical' life.

It will be clear from this discussion that the term 'person' fulfils the same function from the standpoint of the agent as the term 'self' does in traditional philosophy, which thinks from the standpoint of the subject. And since the effect of transferring our point of view from the 'I think' to the 'I do' is to overcome the dualism which is inseparable from the theoretical standpoint, the dualism of a rational and an empirical self disappears. There is no longer any need to isolate the two aspects of unity and difference in an antinomy of sheer identity and sheer difference. A personal being is at once subject and object; but he is both because he is primarily agent. As subject he is 'I', as object he is 'You', since the 'You' is always 'the Other'. The unity of the personal is, then, to be sought in the community of the 'You and I', and since persons are agents, this community is not merely matter of fact, but also matter of intention.

But this is to anticipate. For the moment it is more important to notice that the theory of the personal is philosophical and not scientific. In other words, when we consider the self in its actuality as a personal being we do not initiate an anthropological enquiry. Anthropology is a science, and a scientific enquiry is merely objective; and an objective account is necessarily impersonal. From the traditional standpoint, with its polar opposition of subject and object, we look to science for an account of man, but to philosophy for a theory of the self. When we substitute for this the standpoint of the Agent, we still look to science for an objective account of man. But it is to philosophy we must look for a theory of the personal. The change of standpoint makes no difference to science, but it does make a difference to philosophy and, in consequence, to the philosophical account of science. Science now appears from the philosophical point of view as one of the characteristic reflective activities of the personal; as the deliberate attempt to improve and extend our generalized knowledge of the Other in its otherness. As we have already noticed, this involves a necessary abstraction by limitation of attention. Action cannot be object for a subject; for a purely objective attitude reduces action to behaviour and represents it as matter of fact, not as matter of intention. Now that we have recognized that our change of attitude takes us from the isolated self to the self in relation to the Other, and so to the person as existent, we can express this truth in a more concrete fashion. I exist as an individual only in a personal relation to other individuals. Formally stated, 'I' am one term in the relation 'You and I' which constitutes both the 'I' and the 'You'. But within this relation, which constitutes my existence, I can isolate myself from you in intention, so that my relation to you becomes impersonal. In this event, I treat you as object, refusing the personal relationship. This is always possible because the form of the personal involves its own negation. Impersonality is the negative aspect of the personal; since only a person can behave impersonally, just as only a subject can think objectively.

From this it follows that any objective or impersonal knowledge of the human, any *science* of man, whether psychological or sociological, involves a negation of the personal relation of the 'I' and the 'You', and so of the relation which constitutes them persons. Formally, such knowledge is knowledge of the 'You', that is, of the other person; but not of the other person in personal relation to the knower, but as object in the world. I can know another person *as a person* only by entering into personal relation with him. Without this I can know him only by observation and inference; only objectively. The knowledge which I can obtain in this way is valid knowledge; my conclusions from observations can be true or false, they can be verified or falsified by further observation or by experiment. But it is abstract knowledge, since it constructs its object by limitation of attention to what can be known about other persons without entering into personal relations with them.

The full meaning of this will only become evident at a later stage. But the point is of such importance that we had better guard against an easy misinterpretation from the beginning. I have said that this abstraction from the full personal relationship which makes the 'You' an object for 'Me', is always possible. It would be a mistake to imagine that this implies that it is unjustifiable. It is true that it is not unconditionally justifiable, and therefore it requires justification. The personal relation is constitutive for the personal field and therefore neither requires nor admits of justification. The impersonal relation of persons is, however, the negation of the personal, and is therefore justifiable in so far as it is necessary to the constitution of the personal, which includes its own negative. Since persons are agents and action is intentional, this can only mean that when the impersonal relation is intentional it is justifiable by a relation to a personal intention which includes it. If it is not so controlled, or when it has no such relation, it is unjustifiable.

We can exemplify this point, so far as it concerns our present interest, by reference to the science of psychology. Let us suppose that a teacher of psychology is visited by a pupil who wishes to consult him about the progress of his work. The interview begins as a simple personal conversation between them, and the teacher's attitude to the pupil is a normal personal attitude. As it proceeds, however, it becomes evident that something is wrong with the pupil. He is in an abnormal state of mind, and the psychologist recognizes clear symptoms of hysteria. At once the attitude of the teacher changes. He becomes a professional psychologist, observing and dealing with a classifiable case of mental disorder. From his side the relation has changed from a personal to an impersonal one; he adopts an *objective* attitude, and the pupil takes on the character of an object to be studied, with the purpose of determining the causation of his behaviour. There may be no outward sign of this change; indeed the teacher may deliberately conceal it and pursue the conversation as

29

before. But what he now says is governed by a different intention, a theoretical intention to discover what is the matter with his pupil and what has brought it about.

Now this new attitude of the psychologist's, if we consider it from the point of view of the relation of teacher and pupil, is abnormal; and the departure from the normal attitude is justified, and indeed necessitated by the abnormal behaviour of the pupil. But it is also the normal attitude of a psychologist when pursuing his scientific researches into human behaviour. It is indeed the attitude which makes any activity scientific. We might, therefore, equally well have begun by contrasting the scientific attitude towards human beings with our normal attitude to one another in personal intercourse. On the other hand, we need not have introduced science at all in order to make this contrast. We might have illustrated the impersonal relation and the attitude which it expresses by considering an employer interviewing a candidate for a post, or an examiner conducting a *viva voce* examination, or a judge trying an accused person in a court of law. Even these would be rather special examples of what is, in fact, one of the commonest features of our everyday experience.

What emerges for our present purpose is that our relation to another person may either be personal or impersonal. Like all our relations to the Other, these are primarily practical, but they have, of course, their theoretical aspect. Each, therefore, gives rise to a knowledge of people. The first gives rise to that personal understanding of others which is the result of reflection upon our personal dealings with men and women of varying sorts under varied conditions, and which we sometimes call 'a knowledge of the world'; the second, if it is systematically pursued, leads to the scientific knowledge of man and his behaviour which forms the content of the psychological sciences. These two types of knowledge are different, and indeed contradictory. The one assumes, and implies, that men are free agents, responsible for their behaviour, choosing their mode of action in the light of a distinction between right and wrong; the other that all human behaviour follows determined patterns, and that the laws which we obey are, like those which govern all natural objects, discoverable by objective scientific methods of investigation. This duality of knowledge, personal and impersonal, is the concrete statement of the antimony of freedom and determinism.

Now if we consider these two conceptions from a purely theoretical standpoint, we must ask, since they are incompatible, which of them is the true conception. If we do this, we are likely to conclude that it is the objective, scientific conception which must be accepted as the true one. Indeed, we may say, if it is the objective view, if it is the view which is scientific, then it *must* be the proper view; and if our ordinary, or our traditional view differs from it, we must attribute the difference to the emotional attitudes which are inseparable from our personal contacts with one another, and from the practical need to maintain our own self-esteem. Yet it is precisely an emotional prejudice which underlies and motivates this choice. The term 'objective' does not mean 'true'. Objective statements are often false. Nor is the term 'scientific' synonymous with correct. The tracks of science are littered with scientific theories which have been abandoned as incorrect. If our generation tends to associate truth with science and objectivity, the association rests upon no logical implication, but only upon an emotional prejudice in favour of science.

There is, however, an ambiguity in our use of the term 'emotional' which it is important to clear up at this point. We are apt to contrast the objective attitude which is characteristic of scientific enquiry with other, more personal attitudes, by calling it unemotional. But this is to restrict the proper meaning of the term in a misleading way. Any personal activity must have a motive, and all motives are, in the large sense, emotional. Indeed, an attitude of mind is simply an emotional state. The attitude of a scientist pursuing his vocation is, therefore, an emotional state. It is no doubt an emotional state of a specific kind, and one that has, in certain conditions, to be sustained by a deliberate effort and with difficulty. But if the scientific state of mind were completely free of emotion, scientific enquiry could not be carried on. It would be entirely motiveless, and therefore impossible. Further, if we identify this objective attitude with rationality, then it follows that rationality is itself an emotional state. In contrasting reason with emotion we are under one of the strongest influences in our Western tradition— the Stoic dualism of Reason and the Passions, with its prejudice against being emotionally involved in the results of our actions. When this practical dualism becomes theoretical by the substitution of a theoretical for a practical intention, we generate the modern dualistic attitude in which reason is the unemotional and purely logical activity of the mind which produces knowledge; while emotion is the source of error through the prejudice which is inseparable from it. From this comes the ideal of a purely objective rationality, unaffected by emotion, which intends the truth, the whole truth and nothing but the truth; in contrast with an emotional activity where desires provide the motives for activities which terminate in their satisfaction. This is one aspect of the pervasive dualism of modern thought. Schematically it is a dualism, in this incarnation, of intention and motive. We contrast two forms of behaviour; the one rational or objective, the other subjective and emotional. The first has an intention, but no motive; the second a motive but no intention, since the motive fully accounts for the behaviour which flows from it as a cause determines its effect. Strangely enough, the 'objective' activity is the activity of the logical mind—of the Self as subject; while it is the activity of the objective (or empirical) self which is called 'subjective'. Moreover in its purely objective activity of thinking, in its pure theoretical rationality, the self, as subject, is free (since thinking is purely intentional and has no motive), while the object-self is entirely determined by motives of an emotional character, which cause, and so explain, all its behaviour. In this antimony of freedom and determinism, the antithetical terms are not merely contradictory; they are also correlative, and necessitate one another.

For if there is to be objective knowledge, then the object in its character as object of knowledge must be determinate, and equally the subject, in its activity of knowing, must be excluded from this determination.

We have rejected the theoretical standpoint, however, and are no longer bound by its implications. From the standpoint we have adopted, the account we have to give of the relation between the personal and the impersonal attitudes and the knowledge to which each gives rise, is a different one. We can now rid ourselves effectively of the ghost of the old faculty psychology which still haunts our philosophies; we can insist that all our activities, whether practical or theoretical, have their motives as well as their intentions, and are sustained by an emotional attitude. This is not to say that all our thinking is prejudiced or coloured by emotional bias. It may be true in fact that none of us can escape completely from prejudice. But this is not because an element of emotion is present in all our reflection, nor is it true that if we could get rid entirely of this emotional element we should escape from prejudice. We should, in fact, lose the capacity to think altogether. Uncontrolled feelings, like loose thinking, can lead us into error. But even strong emotions, such as love or hatred or anger, may sharpen the focus of our attention, quicken our apprehension of the object upon which they are directed, and lead to the recognition of truths, and even of facts, which otherwise would have escaped our notice.

The relation of our personal to our impersonal knowledge of other people is primarily and practically the relation of two emotional attitudes to the Other, which provide the motives for two different ways of behaving in relation to the Other, and therefore, in the reflective aspect of action, in conceiving the Other. Now since both attitudes are the attitudes of a person, both are, in this sense, personal attitudes. But if the Other is another person, as attitudes to the Other, the one is personal, while the other is impersonal. If one person treats another person impersonally, he treats him as if he were an object and not a person. He negates the personal character of the other, then,

33

that is to say, his freedom as an agent; and treats him as completely conditioned in his behaviour, as if he were not free but determined. Consequently, the concepts of the other person which arise within the two attitudes contradict one another and lead to an antinomy. But we have only to recall the scheme of the personal, in which a positive contains and is constituted by its own negative, to understand the meaning of this. The impersonal attitude in a personal relation is the negative which is necessarily included in the positive personal attitude, and without which it could not exist. Even in the most personal of relationships the other person is in fact an object for us. We see his movements and his gestures; we hear the sounds he makes; if we did not we could not be aware of him at all. Yet we do not hear mere sounds or see mere movements or gestures. What we apprehend through these are the intentions, the feelings, the thoughts of another person who is in communication with ourselves. The impersonal aspect of the personal relation is always present, and necessarily so. It is not always noticed, yet it may be; and at times it may monopolize our attention so that we miss the meaning of the words he speaks or of the movements he makes. We may, perhaps, express in a general fashion what is here indicated if we say that in a personal relation between persons an impersonal relation is necessarily included and subordinated. The negative is for the sake of the positive. Or, from another point of view, we may say that the relation is intentionally personal, and includes the impersonal as a matter of fact.

The impersonal relation, however, reverses this; for its impersonality is intentional, and to this intention the personal fact is subordinated. The relation of a master to his slave—to take an extreme example—is an impersonal one. It is constituted by the intention of the master to treat the other person 'as a means merely'—to use Kant's phrase; or as Aristotle put it 'as a living tool'. Consequently he regards him not as a person, nor as an agent, but as an object possessing certain capacities and characteristics which make him useful. Amongst these capacities and characteristics are some which are peculiar to persons. What master would consider that an honest slave was no better than a dishonest one? The relation is in fact a relation of persons. The master knows this, and recognizes it as a matter of fact. But the personal characteristics of the slave are subordinated to his own impersonal intention. Certain qualities of character, for example, which he would consider contemptible in a freeman, such as a readiness to suffer insult and injustice without retaliation, he will consider desirable in his slave. We may say, then, that a relation between persons is impersonal when it subordinates the personal aspect to the impersonal; that is to say when the negative dominates and subordinates the positive aspect; when the positive is for the sake of the negative.

We should all agree that slavery is unjustifiable, since it involves a practical denial of human personality. But whether we are right in this or not, it is at least certain that it must require a justification. But a personal relationship of persons does not require justification. It is the norm for all personal relations. If I treat another person as a person and enter into fully personal relations with him, it is absurd to ask me to justify my behaviour. There is therefore an important difference between the personal attitude and the impersonal, and consequently between the conception of the other person that each involves. The former is always right, since it needs no justification; but the latter, since it does require to be justified, is right only conditionally. We have to ask of any impersonal attitude under what conditions it is justifiable. The answer to this question which seems proper is that the impersonal attitude is justifiable when it is itself subordinated to the personal attitude, when it is adopted for the sake of the personal, and is itself included as a negative which is necessary to the positive.

The reasons for this answer will appear at a later point. To illustrate its meaning let us return to the example of the psychologist and his pupil with which we began. The psychologist, we said, recognizing symptoms of neurosis in his pupil's behaviour, changes his attitude from a personal to an impersonal one. The pupil at once becomes, for the psychologist, a case of hysteria to be observed and diagnosed, that is to say, accounted for by reference to its causes. He observes the young man objectively, asking himself, 'What is the matter with him?' as any of us would do in the circumstances. He observes him scientifically, that is to say objectively, and with the knowledge at his disposal of the techniques available for answering the question. Let us then assume that the psychologist undertakes a complete investigation of the case and that the pupil submits to it, and consider the situation that arises.

We must notice first that the objective attitude of the psychologist arises from, and is indeed made necessary by, the abnormal condition of the pupil. For the abnormality consists in his inability to enter into normal personal relations with others. This makes the personal attitude impossible in practice. More specifically, the abnormality consists in a loss of freedom—in a partial inability to act. The behaviour of the neurotic is compulsive. Either he does not know what he is doing, or he cannot help doing it. In either case what has happened is that the motives of his behaviour are no longer under intentional control, and function as 'causes' which determine his activity by themselves. This, at least, is the assumption underlying the change of attitude, the assumption that human behaviour is abnormal or irrational when it can only be understood as the effect of a cause, and not by reference to the intention of an agent.

In the second place, the activity directed by the impersonal attitude is justified only if it falls within and is subordinated to an intention to restore the other person to normal health. This means to rid him of the compulsion which makes his behaviour *merely* caused by restoring intentional control; so that once again personal relations with him become possible, and an impersonal relation unnecessary. It is not difficult to see that this must be so. For suppose that the impersonal attitude were self-justifying and unconditionally right. It would then be normative for the activities which it initiates. In the course of his investigation of the cause of the abnormality, the psychologist might find that this particular case was of unusual interest, presenting novel features which suggested an important modification of current psychological theory. It might well be that this suggestion could only be confirmed if the neurosis were considerably accentuated. In that case, not merely would the psychologist be able to make a case in favour of accentuating his pupil's illness; he would not need to make a case for it, *it would be the right thing for him to do.* If this is preposterous, if it reminds us of certain Nazi doctors of infamous memory, it can only be because we know that a purely objective attitude to another person can only be justified if it falls within and is subordinated to a personal norm. The other person may be treated rightly as a means to the realization of our intentions, and so conceived rightly as an object, only so far as this objective conception is recognized as a negative and subordinate aspect of his existence as a person, and so far as our treatment of him is regulated by this recognition.

These tentative observations are sufficient for our immediate purpose, which is to distinguish, and in distinguishing to relate, the two types of knowledge we possess, and may seek systematically to extend, of the world of persons. The one is our knowledge of persons as persons; the other our knowledge of persons as objects. The first depends upon and expresses a personal attitude to the other person, the second an impersonal attitude. Both types of knowledge can be generalized in reflection; either, that is to say, may give rise to an activity of intellectual reflection governed by a pure reflective intention. In the first case, when the attitude is personal, this reflective activity will be philosophical. In the other it will be scientific. The first will yield a philosophy of the personal; the second a science of man, or in the wide sense of the term, an anthropology. We can now see that the question whether the personal conception of men as free agents or the scientific conception of man as a determined being is the correct one does not arise except through a misunderstanding. Both are correct; and this is possible because they do not refer to the same field. The concept 'man' is a general class concept. Its field of reference is the genus *Homo sapiens*, that is to say, the class of existents which are identifiable by observation, as possessing the factual characteristics by which objects are assigned to this class. The connotation of the term 'man' is those characteristics which all members of the class have, as matter of fact, in common. The concept is therefore an abstract concept, and the field to which it refers is an isolate. It depends upon a limitation of attention, and this limitation of attention is constituted by the impersonal attitude of the observer. The field of anthropology is persons as objects for us; and our objective or scientific knowledge of man is such knowledge of one another as we can obtain without entering into personal relation. All the knowledge of one another which is possible only through personal intercourse is *ipso facto* excluded from consideration.

The concept of 'the personal', on the contrary, is not an exclusive concept, and the field of the personal is not an isolate. It is primarily the field in which we know one another as persons in personal relation. But it includes, as we have seen, the objective knowledge of one another we possess, as the negative aspect of itself which is necessary for its possibility. In this sense, a knowledge of the personal must include an objective knowledge of man, and the work of the anthropological sciences is justified and is, in principle, correct, though of course it may be mistaken in detail. On the other hand, if we take the scientific account as a complete account—as absolute and not relative— so that it entails the rejection of the personal conception, with the freedom which this implies, then we are indeed in error. But the error is not in the scientific account; it does not imply that the scientist should correct his assumption or his conclusions, or that we should reject them. The error lies in our failure to understand the special character of scientific knowledge, and so not in our science but in our philosophy of the personal. It is, in fact, the result of a false valuation of the objective attitude, which makes it normative for all possible attitudes.

38

THE FIELD OF THE PERSONAL

It is of special importance that we should not mistake the ground of this conclusion. It does not rest upon any distinction between subjective and objective entities. It has no relation to the controversy about the objects of psychology, whether they are observable or not, by introspection or otherwise; whether introspection is really retrospection, and therefore for some reason suspect. We may recall an earlier conclusion of our own that the object of reflection is always the past; so that all reflective observation, in physics as in psychology, is retrospective. It does not matter, for our purpose, whether thoughts, images, perceivings, rememberings and so on are 'private' occurrences or not. The distinction we have drawn between a personal and an 'objective' knowledge of one another rests upon this, that all objective knowledge is knowledge of matter of fact only and necessarily excludes any knowledge of what is matter of intention. What is intended is never matter of fact, though it may be a fact that I intend it. For what is intended is always future, and there are no future facts; though again it may be a fact that something which I anticipate will, in fact, happen. But it may not: my expectation may not be fulfilled; I may fail to realize my intention. In that case not merely is it not matter of fact, but it never will be. If it does become matter of fact, then it has already happened; it is no longer intended, but apprehended retrospectively.

In general this means, for our present purpose, that an objective knowledge of other persons cannot treat them as agents, but only as determinate objects, that is, as continuants. Determinism is therefore a necessary postulate of the scientific enquiry, and serves not merely to dictate its methodology, but also to isolate the aspect of personal behaviour which is amenable to the method. The method is, as we have seen, to search for patterns of behaviour which recur without change, and to formulate these in 'laws' of general application. The underlying postulate is the postulate of determinism—which is the basis of induction—that the patterns are constants, that they will be found in the behaviour of all members of the class and that they will continue without change in the future *unless there is an interference.*

Conclusions   We may now sum up our conclusion. The field of the personal, with which we are concerned, is defined by a personal attitude to other persons; the field of the anthropological sciences by an impersonal attitude. These two attitudes are primarily practical, though each has its own negative or reflective aspect. The personal attitude is the attitude we adopt when we enter into personal relation with others and treat them as persons. Its reflective aspect, systematically pursued, is a philosophical knowledge of the personal. The impersonal attitude is the one in which we do not treat other people as persons in personal relation with ourselves, but as *men*, that is as members of a determinate class of objects in our environment whose presence and behaviour limits, and so helps or hinders the realization of our own personal ends, and of whom we must take account, since their presence conditions our own actions. This, too, has its reflective aspect in a knowledge which, when methodically developed, provides a science, or set of sciences of human behaviour.

These two types of knowledge—the philosophical and the scientific—are related as the attitudes which sustain them. Both are personal attitudes, in the sense that only a person is capable of adopting either. The impersonal attitude is personal when referred to the 'I' but impersonal when referred to the 'You'. It is indeed the negative aspect of the 'I-You' relationship—an impersonal relation of persons. It is, therefore, included in the personal attitude as a necessary but negative and subordinate aspect of it. It follows that the scientific knowledge of man is included and subordinated, as a negative aspect, in the philosophical knowledge of the personal. Both types of knowledge, therefore, are really knowledge. But the philosophical is knowledge of persons as persons, and therefore as agents; it is the full and inclusive knowledge of the personal other, for to be an agent a person must also be a continuant object in the world. The scientific knowledge is, however, limited and abstract. It is knowledge of the personal other in so far as he is a determinate object, and so as he appears to a mere observer. And since it is the objective or scientific attitude that is limited and subordinate, the personal knowledge is normal for the objective, and self-justifying; while the objective is for the sake of the personal and is justified only in its proper subordination to the personal.

There is then no necessary contradiction between personal freedom and scientific determinism in the anthropological field. The 'I do' is indubitable, and to assert it is to assert my freedom as an agent. But when I do this I make no preposterous claim that I can do anything and everything at will and unconditionally. Every actual action is conditioned, both by the determinate nature of the world in which it must be done and by my own determinate nature as an object in that world. Without this determination I could not act at all, and so could have no freedom. If then I abstract this determinate aspect of action by limitation of attention, and seek to understand it, the scientific method is the correct one, and the only possible one.

If, however, the two types of knowledge were in contradiction with one another, then it would be the scientific account which would have to be rejected. For if it were taken as a complete account, and not as the true account of an aspect, it would be self-contradictory. For it would then have to deny the possibility of the personal activity which produces and possesses it. The 'I' can never depersonalize itself, even if it can depersonalize its attitude to the 'You'. It cannot objectify its own activity of objectification. This would be obvious were it not for our way of talking about science. The logical analysts do well to warn us of the traps that language sets for us. This is one of them, and one which is having an increasingly deleterious effect upon much contemporary thought. We not only objectify science as an entity but personify it, endowing it with personal attributes. 'Science', we say, 'has proved this', or 'has discovered that', or 'has shown that religion rests on a mistake'. Now strictly—and in this context strictness is essential—there is no such thing as 'science' and what is sometimes referred to as the scientific view of the world is either a pure fiction of the imagination, or else a half-baked philosophy which many scientists would reject, and which no scientist, *qua* scientist, is competent to judge.

The term 'science' refers primarily to a personal activity of intellectual reflection. It is something that people do. It means secondarily and negatively the set of beliefs which form the datum for this activity, at a particular time, in any branch of scientific enquiry. All scientific knowledge rests on a postulate of determinism. If it did not, it would not be 'objective'. But if scientific knowledge were made normal for all possible knowledge; if this were interpreted to mean that there are in fact no human activities, or no aspects of human activity which are not objectively determined; if it involved a total denial of freedom, then the possibility of the personal activity which we call science would itself be denied. For the production of science is one of the manifestations of the 'I do'. It is itself matter of intention, and not merely matter of fact.

Finally, the generalization of the impersonal attitude in the anthropological sciences is justified by a practical necessity. In the particular case which we used to illustrate the emergence of an impersonal or objective attitude, the necessity lay in an abnormality in the other person which made the continuance of a personal attitude, already established, impossible. But there is another necessity which applies to the relations between normal persons. The personal relation with the other is possible only between persons who know one another. But our own personal activities depend upon the personal activities of large numbers of people whom we do not and cannot know. All my activities have an economic aspect, for example. I need food; consequently I depend upon a host of people who produce, transport and deliver my food to me. When I pay for my food; I contribute my quota of assistance to the personal lives of all these people. One aspect of my dependence is my belief that their personal activities will continue in the future as they have done in the past. I must trust in the continuance of patterns of habitual activity carried on by persons whom I do not and cannot know.

The relation so established between myself and them is a relation of persons. But the relation is necessarily impersonal; and consequently the knowledge on which it rests must be merely objective. I must conceive the activities of those others upon whom I depend as automatic and continuant, although I know well enough that they are personal doings. In particular, the *organization* of personal activities depends on an objective and impersonal knowledge.

This set of considerations leads to our first major division of the field of the personal. We must distinguish between the direct and the indirect relations of persons. This distinction is not the same as that between the impersonal and personal attitudes, though it has a relation to it. It is a distinction within the field of our enquiry. Direct relations are those which involve a personal acquaintance with one another on the part of the persons related. Indirect relations exclude this condition: they are relations between persons who are not personally known to one another. All indirect relations are therefore necessarily impersonal. Direct relations are those which may or may not be personal, at the will of the persons related. If they are maintained at an impersonal level, this requires a justification. If they are fully personal, they yet necessarily contain a subordinate impersonal aspect.

We shall consider first the direct relations of persons; and we shall begin, in the next chapter, where all human experience begins, with infancy. In this way we may hope to discover the original structure of the personal, and the pattern of its personal development.

CHAPTER TWO

Mother and Child

There is a widespread belief, of which Aristotle is probably the original source, that the human infant is an animal organism which becomes rational, and acquires a human personality, in the process of growing up. In Aristotle's terminology, the baby is *potentially* but not *actually* rational. It realizes this potentiality through a process of habit-formation; and in this process a 'character' is formed. 'Character' is an orderly organization of the original animal impulses, so that they no longer function independently as motives of behaviour, but as elements in a system. Thus the mature human being acts for the satisfaction of his character, of himself as a whole in a whole life, and this satisfaction we call 'happiness'. The child, like the animal, acts for the satisfaction of isolated impulses as they arise, and this satisfaction is 'pleasure'. We might then illustrate the characteristic difference between rational and non-rational behaviour by saying that when an animal is hungry it goes in search of food; but when a man is hungry he looks at his watch to see how long it will be before his next meal.

The Aristotelian theory interests us only because of the influence it has had, and still has, upon our customary ways of thinking. If the notion that children are little animals who acquire the characteristics of rational humanity through education, whose personalities are 'formed' by the pressures brought to bear upon them as they grow up—if this notion seems to us simple common sense, and matter of everyday observation—it is because we share the traditional outlook and attitude of a culture which has been moulded by Greek and in particular by

Aristotelian ideas. So much of common sense is the relic of past philosophies!

Whatever its origin, this view is radically false; and our first task is to uncover the error on which it rests and to replace it by a more adequate view. In his important contribution to psychotherapeutic theory, *The Origin of Love and Hate*, the late Dr. Ian Suttie asserted roundly that the human infant is less like an animal than the human adult.[1] This goes too far, perhaps, in the opposite direction, but it is a valuable corrective to the traditional view. The root of the error is the attempt to understand the field of the personal on a biological analogy, and so through organic categories. The Greek mode of thought was naturally biological, or zoomorphic. The Greek tradition has been strongly reinforced by the organic philosophies of the nineteenth century and the consequent development of evolutionary biology. This in turn led to the attempt to create evolutionary sciences in the human field, particularly in its social aspect. The general result of these convergent cultural activities—the Romantic movement, the organic philosophies, idealist or realist, and evolutionary science—was that contemporary thought about human behaviour, individual and social, became saturated with biological metaphors, and moulded itself to the requirements of an organic analogy. It became the common idiom to talk of ourselves as organisms and of our societies as organic structures; to refer to the history of society as an evolutionary process and to account for all human action as an adaptation to environment.

It was assumed, and still is assumed in many quarters, that this way of conceiving human life is scientific and empirical and therefore the truth about us. It is in fact not empirical; it is *a priori* and analogical. Consequently it is not, in the strict sense, even scientific. For this concept, and the categories of understanding which go with it, were not discovered by a patient unbiased examination of the facts of human activity. They were discovered, at best, through an empirical and scientific study of

[1] Suttie, op. cit., p. 15.

the facts of plant and animal life. They were applied by analogy to the human field on the *a priori* assumption that human life must exhibit the same structure.

The practical consequences are in the end disastrous; but they do reveal the erroneous character of the assumption. To affirm the organic conception in the personal field is implicitly to deny the possibility of action; yet the meaning of the conception lies in its reference to action. We can only act upon the organic conception by transforming it into a determinant of our intention. It becomes an ideal to be achieved. We say, in effect, 'Society is organic; therefore let us make it organic, as it ought to be.' The contradiction here is glaring. If society is organic, then it is meaningless to say that it *ought* to be. For if it ought to be, then it is *not*. The organic conception of the human, as a practical ideal, is what we now call the totalitarian state. It rests on the practical contradiction which corresponds to this theoretical one. 'Man is not free,' it runs, 'therefore he ought not to be free.' If organic theory overlooks human freedom, organic practice must suppress it.

It is one of the major intentions which animate this book to help towards the eradication of this fundamental and dangerous error. It may therefore be advisable, at this point, to issue a flat denial, without qualifications. We are not organisms, but persons. The nexus of relations which unites us in a human society is not organic but personal. Human behaviour cannot be understood, but only caricatured, if it is represented as an adaptation to environment; and there is no such process as social evolution but, instead, a history which reveals a precarious development and possibilities both of progress and of retrogression. It is true, as we have argued already, that the personal necessarily includes an organic aspect. But it cannot be defined in terms of its own negative; and this organic aspect is continuously qualified by its inclusion, so that it cannot even be properly abstracted except through a prior understanding of the personal structure in which it is an essential, though subordinate component. A descent from the personal is possible, in theory and indeed in practice; but there is no way for thought to ascend from the organic to the personal. The organic conception of man excludes, by its very nature, all the characteristics in virtue of which we are human beings. To include them we must change our categories and start afresh from the beginning.

We start then where all human life starts, with infancy; at the stage of human existence where, if at all, we might expect to find a biological conception adequate. If it is not adequate to explain the behaviour of a new-born child, than *a fortiori* it must be completely inadequate as an account of human life in its maturity. The most obvious fact about the human infant is his total helplessness. He has no power of locomotion, nor even of co-ordinated movement. The random movements of limbs and trunk and head of which he is capable do not even suggest an unconscious purposiveness. The essential physiological rhythms are established, and perhaps a few automatic reflexes. Apart from these, he has no power of behaviour; he cannot respond to any external stimulus by a reaction which would help to defend him from danger or to maintain his own existence. In this total helplessness, and equally in the prolonged period of time which must elapse before he can fend for himself at all, the baby differs from the young of all animals. Even the birds are not helpless in this sense. The chicks of those species which nest at a distance from their food supply must be fed by their parents till they are able to fly. But they peck their way out of the egg, and a lapwing chick engaged in breaking out of the shell will respond to its mother's danger call by stopping its activity and remaining quite still.

We may best express this negative difference, with reference to biological conceptions, by saying that the infant has no instincts. That human beings have no instincts is, I understand, a conclusion at which many psychologists have arrived, and to which psychology as a whole increasingly tends. That this has been a slow process arises from the vagueness of the term instinct. If we insist on defining it in terms of strict biological usage, the conclusion follows at once. An eminent biologist to whom I once

referred the question even doubted whether there were any un-
ambiguous instances of instinctive behaviour among the higher
animals. For our purpose we may define the term instinct as a
specific adaptation to environment which does not require to be
learned. The term 'specific' here means 'sufficiently definite to
fulfil its biological function'. A 'specific' adaptation is a response
to an external stimulus which is biologically adequate, which
does not require to be completed, though it may be improved,
by any process of learning. If this is what we mean by 'instinct'
then it is clear that we are born with none. All purposive human
behaviour has to be learned. To begin with, our responses to
stimulus are, without exception, biologically random.

There must, however, be a positive side to this. The baby
must be fitted by nature at birth to the conditions into which
he is born; for otherwise he could not survive. He is, in fact,
'adapted', to speak paradoxically, to being unadapted,
'adapted' to a complete dependence upon an adult human
being. He is made to be cared for. He is born into a love-
relationship which is inherently personal. Not merely his personal development, but his very survival depends upon the
maintaining of this relation; he depends for his existence, that is
to say, upon intelligent understanding, upon rational foresight.
He cannot think for himself, yet he cannot do without thinking;
so someone else must think for him. He cannot foresee his own
needs and provide for them; so he must be provided for by
another's foresight. He cannot do himself what is necessary to
his own survival and development. It must be done for him by
another who can, or he will die.

The baby's 'adaptation' to his 'environment' consists in his
capacity to express his feelings of comfort or discomfort; of
satisfaction and dissatisfaction with his condition. Discomfort he
expresses by crying; comfort by gurgling and chuckling, and
very soon by smiling and crowing. The infant's cry is a call for
help to the mother, an intimation that he needs to be cared for.
It is the mother's business to interpret his cry, to discover by
taking thought whether he is hungry, or cold, or being pricked

by a pin, or ill; and having decided what is the matter with him, to do for him what he needs. If she cannot discover what is the matter, she will consult someone else, or send for the doctor. His expression of satisfaction is closely associated with being cared for, with being nursed, with the physical presence of the mother, and particularly with physical contact. It would seem to be, from a biological point of view, unnecessary. There is no obvious utilitarian purpose in it; for the cessation of his cries would be enough to tell the mother that her efforts had succeeded in removing his distress. It seems impossible to account for it except as an expression of satisfaction in the relation itself; in being touched caressingly, attended to and cared for by the mother. This is evidence that the infant has a need which is not simply biological but personal, a need to be in touch with the mother, and in conscious perceptual relation with her. And it is astonishing at what an early age a baby cries not because of any physiological distress, but because he has noticed that he is alone, and is upset by his mother's absence. Then the mere appearance of the mother, or the sound of her voice, is enough to remove the distress and turn his cries into smiles of satisfaction.

Now if we attend to these everyday facts without any theoretical prejudice, it is obvious that the relation of mother and child is quite inadequately expressed in biological terms, and that the attempt to give an organic account of it must lead to a caricature. For to talk of the infant's behaviour as an adaptation to environment ought to mean that it responds to external stimuli in a way that is biologically effective. Yet it is precisely his inability to do this that is the governing factor. Further, when we speak of 'environment' in a biological context, we mean nature, as the source of stimuli and of material for the supply of the organism's needs as well as of dangers to its survival. But the human infant is not in direct relation to nature. His environment is a home, which is not a natural habitat, but a human creation, an institution providing in advance for human needs, biological and personal, through human foresight and artifice. In general, to represent the process of human development, even at its earliest stage, as an organic process, is to represent it in terms which are equally applicable to the development of animals, and therefore to exclude reference to any form of behaviour which is exclusively human; to exclude reference to rationality in any of its expressions, practical or theoretical; reference to action or to knowledge, to deliberate purpose or reflective thought. If this were correct, no infant could ever survive. For its existence and its development depend from the beginning on rational activities, upon thought and action. The baby cannot yet think or act. Consequently he must depend for his life upon the thought and action of others. The conclusion is not that the infant is still an animal which will become rational through some curious organic process of development. It is that he cannot, even theoretically, live an isolated existence; that he is not an independent individual. He lives a common life as one term in a personal relation. Only in the process of development does he learn to achieve a relative independence, and that only by appropriating the techniques of a rational social tradition. All the infant's activities in maintaining his existence are shared and co-operative. He cannot even feed; he has to be fed. The sucking reflex is his sole contribution to his own nutrition, the rest is the mother's.

If we insist on interpreting the facts through biological categories, we shall be committed to talking puerilities about maternal instinct. There is no such thing, of course; if there were, it would have to include some very curious instinctive components, such as a shopping instinct and a dressmaking instinct. Even the term 'mother' in this connection is not a biological term. It means simply the adult who cares for the baby. Usually it will be the woman who bore him, but this is not necessarily so. A human infant does not necessarily die, like an animal, if his mother dies in childbirth. The mother may be an aunt, or an elder sister or a hired nurse. She need not even be a female. A man can do all the mothering that is necessary, if he is provided with a feeding-bottle, and learns how to do it in precisely the same fashion that a woman must learn.

From all this it follows that the baby is not an animal organism, but a person, or in traditional terms, a rational being. The reason is that his life, and even his bodily survival, depends upon intentional activity, and therefore upon knowledge. If nobody intends his survival and acts with intention to secure it, he cannot survive. That he cannot act intentionally, that he cannot even think for himself and has no knowledge by which to live is true, and is of the first importance. It does not signify, however, that he is merely an animal organism; if it did it would mean that he could live by the satisfaction of organic impulse, by reaction to stimulus, by instinctive adaptation to his natural environment. But this is totally untrue. He cannot live at all by any initiative, whether personal or organic, of his own. He can live only through other people and in dynamic relation with them. In virtue of this fact he is a person, for the personal is constituted by the relation of persons. His rationality is already present, though only germinally, in the fact that he lives and can only live by communication. His essential natural endowment is the impulse to communicate with another human being. Perhaps his cry of distress when he wakens alone in the night in his cot in the nursery has no meaning for *him*, but for the mother it has; and as she hurries to him she will respond to it by calling, 'It's all right, darling, mother's coming.'

We can now realize why it is that the activities of an infant, taken as a whole, have a personal and not an organic form. They are not merely motivated, but their motivation is governed by intention. The intention is the mother's, necessarily; the motives, just as necessarily, are the baby's own. The infant is active; if his activities were unmotivated, he would be without any consciousness, and could not even develop a capacity to see or hear. But if he is hungry, he does not begin to feed or go in search of food. His feeding occurs at regular intervals, as part of a planned routine, just as an adult's does. The satisfaction of his motives is governed by the mother's intention. It is part of the routine of family life. Now it is important for us to gain some reliable idea of the structure of personal motivation—in distinction from intention; and since motive and intention operate, in the case of the infant, in different persons, and the baby has no intention of his own, we can do this most easily by studying the original motivational endowment of persons in infancy, before going on to consider the processes of its development. We must ask ourselves, therefore, at this point, what the structure of personal motivation is, as it manifests itself in babyhood.

We can dismiss at once any notion that we are born with a set of 'animal' impulses which later take on a rational form. There is no empirical evidence for anything like this, and it is inherently improbable. In the absence of intention and knowledge, consciousness is motive, as we have seen. This means primarily that a feeling is present which selects the movement which responds to a stimulus. In the absence of any behaviour on the part of an organism, that is, of any activity which is so directed that we can understand it as an adaptation to the environment, we have no ground even for suspecting the existence of a motive, or indeed of consciousness at all. A motive is an element in, or aspect of, a behavioural activity. A specific motive means a specific form of behaviour. To say that any living creature is endowed with a set of motives can only mean that it behaves in a set of distinguishable ways, and that its behaviour is of a kind which requires us to postulate a conscious component.

Now so far as concerns behaviour which is adapted to a natural environment, the human infant does not behave at all. Its movements are conspicuously random. If this were all, we should have no grounds for suspecting the presence of motives, or indeed of consciousness. The baby's movements could quite well be described as automatisms. What prevents this conclusion is an observable progress, with no conspicuous breaks, in the direction of controlled activity. The movements gradually lose their random character and acquire direction and form. But the character of this development is quite unlike that observable even in the highest animals. It does not rapidly produce a capacity to adapt itself to the environment. In the early stages, at least, it does not seem to tend in this direction at all. It is quite a long time before the baby learns to walk or to stand or even to crawl; and his early locomotion, so far from making him more capable of looking after himself, increases the dangers of his existence, and the need for constant parental care and watchfulness. Nature leaves the provision for his physiological needs and his well-being to the mother for many years, until indeed he has learned to form his own intentions, and acquired the skill to execute them and the knowledge and foresight which will enable him to act responsibly as a member of a personal community.

The child's progress appears rather to consist in the acquirement of skills, as it were for their own sake, without any distinguishable objective to which they are a means; and the primary stage seems to be concerned with the use of the organs of sense. The baby learns first to discriminate colours and shapes, and to distinguish familiar from unfamiliar complexes of these. Similarly he acquires the skill to distinguish sounds and concatenations of sounds, and to make different sounds at will. Then he learns to correlate sight and touch, acquiring the skill to put his hand on what he sees. In this stage he is learning to discriminate in awareness; acquiring the basic skills which are essential for an awareness of objects, that is, for sense-perception. Because sense-perception is learned so early in life we are very apt to forget that it has to be learned at all; so that we talk of it as though the power to perceive a world of objects were born in us, and that its 'immediacy' is an original datum of human experience. This is not so. Perceiving by means of the senses is an acquired skill, and varies from one person to the next, partly no doubt because of inherited physiological differences; but partly, and probably in most cases to a much larger extent, because some of us carry the process of learning to use our senses farther than others.

We need not attempt to follow this progress in detail. Only a few general observations are necessary for our purpose. We must first notice the hierarchical and systematic character of the process. The child must first learn the simplest elementary skills whether of sensory discrimination or of movement. His attention, and therefore his consciousness, is concentrated, at any stage, upon acquiring the particular skill he is learning. The learning process is a conscious process. But when a particular lesson has been learned, the child's attention passes beyond it to the acquirement of a wider skill, in which the skill already learned is a component. What he has already learnt to do can now be done without attention, automatically; while attention is directed to learning a new skill for which the first provides an unconscious basis. He must learn to stand before he can learn to walk; to discriminate sounds and to produce articulate sounds before he can learn to speak. Each lower-level skill becomes thus the automatic basis of a higher-level skill to be acquired. In this way a hierarchical system of skills is developed, the lower levels of which support the higher skills automatically as unconscious components.

This process is usually—and rightly—described as the formation of habits, and the integrated system of skills is a system of habits. In an earlier discussion we recognized habit as the negative aspect of an action; as that in action which is not intended because not attended to. It is included in, and governed by intention, but in itself it has an organic character. It is reaction to stimulus. Bearing this in mind, we see that in human behaviour habit takes the place of instinct in animals. It functions in human activity as an instinct does in animal activity. The essential difference is that a habit is consciously acquired. It is a learned response to stimulus, while an instinct is a response to stimulus which does not have to be learned. But this difference carries an important corollary. What has been learned can, in principle, be unlearned and relearned. If this is not in fact the case, particularly with the basic habits which are acquired very early, it is because the changing of a habit is a deliberate and conscious process, which requires a sufficient motive to sustain it; and also because to unlearn a basic habit involves a cessation of all those higher-level activities in which it is an automatic component. It is this functional correspondence of personal habit and animal instinct which lies at the root of the widespread tendency to describe certain kinds of human behaviour as instinctive. It would, however, be less misleading to reverse the tendency and to speak of animal instincts as innate habits.

We may notice next that this aspect of the child's development has the character of play. Play is activity carried on for its own sake. It is not, however, random but directed activity. It has a goal; but the goal is for the sake of the activity. Play is therefore essentially concerned with skill—with its acquirement, its improvement, and its manifestation. The goal is not *substantially* intended; it functions rather as a test or verification of the skill. We contrast it with work, which is activity in which skill is not merely displayed but used; in which the interest centres in the goal to be achieved, while the skilled expenditure of energy is merely a means to the end, for the sake of this end and therefore normally automatic and unconscious. But the play of children and young animals, though it is, in this fashion, activity for its own sake, is not therefore functionless. When seen in relation to the life of the individual as a whole, it is clearly an exercise or a practising of skills which are necessary as means to the mature activities of later life. The young imitate in play the necessary activities of maturity; so that their play is a way of learning adult skills. But there is a great difference between children's play and that of animals. The child is learning the life of a personal maturity; the animal a life of biological maturity. The difference is a difference in form, not merely in degree of complexity. We need call attention only to a few of the differences. First, animals in play are, in general, practising and so perfecting skills which are in some sense already present from the beginning. The child has to start from scratch, and has to learn everything. All his skills are acquired. Secondly, the child's acquiring of skills is a cumulative process. Simple skills are used in acquiring more complex skills, and the process goes on indefinitely. For in learning them he learns how to learn.

Thirdly, at an early stage of the process we begin to suspect the presence of deliberate intention, and soon we are sure of it. The form of the child's behaviour convinces us that he knows what he is doing. Opinions will differ as to the point at which a mere reaction to stimulus gives place to deliberate action; at which the child can form an intention and so foresee the end which is his goal, and select a means of attaining it. We can be sure, however, that it does not come as a sudden miraculous intrusion; and that it has been present for some time before we can verify its presence as observers. Indeed it would be methodologically correct, even if not empirically necessary, to assume its presence from the beginning, or at least of some capacity of which it is a manifestation, and which expresses itself in overt behaviour as soon as the conditions permit.

This leads us to consider the last of the differences from animal learning to which we must refer. Intention involves knowledge, and knowledge depends upon the acquirement of reflective skills. The basic reflective skill, on which the others depend, is imagination; the formation, definition and co-ordination of images, especially visual and auditory images. Hand in hand with this there goes the discrimination of feelings, particularly those which are associated with tactual experience; and the co-ordination of these with sensory images. This development of imagination is primarily, no doubt, a negative aspect of the practical skills we have already considered. But there is also a play of the imagination in which the reflective skills are acquired and exercised for their own sake. We call this phantasy. An important part of the child's play activity is therefore the development of a life of phantasy for its own sake, which is not governed by logic—that is to say, by a practical reference to the Other—but by feeling. There is no good reason to suppose that any but the lowest stage of this acquirement of reflective skills is present in any of the animals.

Finally, we must return to our starting-point, from which this discussion of the child's development took its rise. We set out to discover the general principles of an original motivation for

human behaviour. Instead, we have talked about the development of habits, laying stress upon the contrast with animal
development. For this there were two reasons. The first was that
the infant's helplessness, and the random character of its earliest
movements, seem hardly to require the presence of a motive
consciousness to account for them. But when we consider the
development which has its origin in these random movements,
particularly the continuity and the hierarchical character of
their gradual determination as a system of habit, we are forced
to conclude that a motivating consciousness is present from the
beginning. Automatic reflexes do not develop. They remain
with us throughout life in their original form. At most we
acquire in some cases a precarious ability to suppress them by
deliberate effort. The random character of the movements at the
start, if it is the beginning of a process of definition and discrimination, must be motivated by a consciousness which is
itself as indefinite as awareness can be. Our earlier analysis of
consciousness[1] enables us to give a meaning to this. The infant's
original consciousness, even as regards its sensory elements,
must be feeling, and feeling at its most primitive and undiscriminated level. What it cannot be is a set of discriminated
'animal impulses', each with its implicit reference to a mode of
behaviour, in relation to the environment, which would satisfy
them. We have no ground for thinking that the new-born child
can distinguish between a feeling of pain, a feeling of sickness
and a feeling of hunger. This discrimination, too, we must
assume, has to be learned. The most we have a right to assert,
on the empirical evidence, is an original capacity to distinguish,
in feeling, between comfort and discomfort. We postulate, therefore, an original feeling consciousness, with a discrimination
between positive and negative phases.

The second reason for introducing this excursus on the
development of skills is that it has only a negative importance
for our main subject. It is essential that it should be considered,
if only to show that it is not being overlooked. It is important to

[1] *The Self as Agent*, pp. 119 ff.

57

bear it in mind throughout, if we are not to fall into the error of giving a 'subjective' account of the personal, and so implying the dualism which we have found good reason to reject. But the acquiring of skills, the formation of a system of habits, is only the negative aspect of personal development. Skill is always for the sake of an end beyond it to which it is a means; and even where fully intentional action is required for the formation of a habit, once formed it becomes automatic; attention passes beyond it and it functions as a reaction to stimulus which supports action and is included within action. The progress in skilled behaviour which we have discussed is, then, only the negative aspect of the child's personal development. Habit, we discovered earlier, as the negative aspect of action, has an organic structure; it is reaction to stimulus. We have therefore been considering the organic aspect of the child's development. For this reason the enthusiast for biological explanation will be tempted to refer to animal analogies at every point and to retort that the differences are merely in complexity, and are open, in principle, to organic formulation. This may be admitted. In the same way, physiological processes are open, in principle, to chemical formulation, through a proper selection of their negative aspect; and the movements of the planets can, in principle, be accounted for on the Ptolemaic hypothesis, though the complexity of the account, and the amount of imaginative ingenuity it would involve, would render it suspect even if it were given.

We selected this negative aspect of the infant's life by the simple device of thinking of him as an isolate, and seeking the origin of his behaviour wholly within himself; by treating him as a self-contained individual. In particular, we referred the form of his behaviour wholly to him. But we have already noted that this is not correct. The form of his behaviour is governed by the intention of the mother, in terms of a personal mode of corporate life into which it must be fitted. Because of this even the negative aspect of the child's development has a rational form, although the intention which rationalizes it has to be, for a considerable time, wholly the mother's. The consequence is that the skills a child acquires, and the form in which he acquires them, fit him to take his place as a member of a personal community, and not to fend for himself in natural surroundings.

The whole of this aspect of human development, then, falls within and helps to constitute its positive aspect. It falls, that is, within the 'You and I' of the mother-child relation. For the mother plays with the child, and the child responds; the child calls for the participation, or at least the attention of the adult, and for the admiration and approval of his success. His play has another character which we omitted to mention. It is not merely an *exercise*, but a *display* of skill. The reference to the mother is pervasive in all the child's activities. He does not merely learn, as animals do, by instinct helped out by trial and error; he is *taught*. *His* acquirement of skills is an education. It is a co-operative process which requires from the start the foresight, judgment and action of a mature person to give it an intentional form. Because of this, the child's development has a continuous reference to the distinction between 'right' and 'wrong'. He learns to await the right time for the satisfaction of his desires; that some activities are permitted and others suppressed; that some things may be played with and others not. He learns, in general, to submit his impulses to an order imposed by another will than his; and to subordinate his own desires to those of another person. He learns, in a word, to submit to reason.

Now the original capacity to feel comfort and discomfort, which we admitted, is a psychological abstraction. It exists only as the motive consciousness of a pattern of behaviour—an original 'adaptation' to the conditions of life. But the total helplessness of the infant makes any directed movement in relation to the environment out of the question. His feeling of comfort or discomfort is, indeed, the motive of an activity of expression, the function of which is to communicate his feeling to the mother, and to elicit a response from her. When he feels uncomfortable he cries; and his cry is an unconscious call for assistance. The mother understands it so, and responds to it by comforting him.

It has commonly been asserted that what distinguishes us from the animals is the gift of speech. There is an obvious truth in this, but it has two defects if used for purposes of definition. The power of speech is sometimes defined as the capacity to express ourselves. This misses an essential point; for the power of speech is as much the capacity to understand what is said to us as it is to say things to other people. The ability to speak is then, in the proper sense, the capacity to enter into reciprocal communication with others. It is our ability to share our experience with one another and so to constitute and participate in a common experience. Secondly, speech is a particular skill; and like all skills it presupposes an end to which it is a means. No one considers that deaf-mutes lack the characteristic which distinguishes them as human beings from the animals. They are merely obliged to discover other means of communication than speech. Long before the child learns to speak he is able to communicate, meaningfully and intentionally, with his mother. In learning language, he is acquiring a more effective and more elaborate means of doing something which he already can do in a crude and more primitive fashion. If this were not so, not merely the child's acquiring of speech, but the very existence of language would be an inexplicable mystery. Nor should we forget that he learns to speak by being spoken to; he is taught to speak, and he understands what is said to him before he is able to respond in articulate words.

It would, of course, be possible to find, in animal life, instances in plenty which seem to be, and perhaps actually are, cases of communication. To take these as objections to what has been urged here would be to miss the point. For these are not definitive. In the human infant—and this is the heart of the matter—the impulse to communication is his sole adaptation to the world into which he is born. Implicit and unconscious it may be, yet it is sufficient to constitute the mother-child relation as the basic form of human existence, as a personal mutuality, as a 'You and I' with a common life. For this reason the infant is born a person and not an animal. All his subsequent experience, all the habits he forms and the skills he acquires fall within this framework, and are fitted to it. Thus human experience is, in principle, shared experience; human life, even in its most individual elements, is a common life; and human behaviour carries always, in its inherent structure, a reference to the personal Other. All this may be summed up by saying that the unit of personal existence is not the individual, but two persons in personal relation; and that we are persons not by individual right, but in virtue of our relation to one another. The personal is constituted by personal relatedness. The unit of the personal is not the 'I', but the 'You and I'.

We can now define the original motivation-pattern of personal behaviour. We have recognized, as the minimum of our original motive consciousness, the capacity to feel comfort and discomfort. But the behaviour which is motived by this distinction is, we now see, an activity which communicates the experience to the mother. The motivation of the infant's behaviour is still bipolar; it has a positive and a negative phase; the negative phase being genetically prior, since it expresses a need for the mother's aid, while the positive expresses satisfaction in the supply of its needs. But both the negative and positive poles have an original and implicit reference to the other person, with whom the infant shares a common life. This original reference to the other is of a definitive importance. It is the germ of rationality. For the character that distinguishes rational from non-rational experience, in all the expressions of reason, is its reference to the Other-than-myself. What we call 'objectivity' is one expression of this—the conscious reference of an idea to an object. But it is to be noted that this is not the primary expression of reason. What is primary, even in respect of reflective thought—is the reference to the other *person*. A true judgment is one which is made by one individual—as every judgment must be—but is valid for all others. Objective thought presupposes this by the assumption that there is a *common* object about which a communication may be made.

The human infant, then, being born into, and adapted to, a

common life with the mother, is a person from birth. His survival depends upon reason, that is to say, upon action and not upon reaction to stimulus. We must, therefore, complete our analysis by defining it in its positive personal mode, which contains and is constituted by its negative or organic aspect. The animal has certain needs—for food, for warmth, for protection. It is endowed by nature with specific patterns of behaviour for their satisfaction. The child has the same needs; but it is not so provided. Instead, it has a single need which contains them all—the need for a mother, the need to be cared for. If this need is satisfied the organic needs are provided for. The baby does not feed himself, he is fed. He does not protect himself, he is protected. The provision for his various needs falls within the mother's care as aspects and manifestations of it. They differentiate her caring and give it actuality and systematic form. The baby need do nothing about his organic needs, and therefore need not even be aware of them discriminatingly. Now the positive motive of the mother's caring is her love for the child; it contains, however, and subordinates a negative component of fear—anxiety for the child's welfare. This negative component is essential, since it provides the motive for thought and foresight on the child's behalf, and for provision in advance against the dangers to its life, health and welfare, both in the present and the future. Without it love would be inoperative and ineffectual, a mere sentimentality and therefore unreal.

Now since the mother-child relation is the original unit of personal existence, the motivation of the child's behaviour must be reciprocal, even if this reciprocity is, to begin with, merely implicit. The positive and negative poles of the infant's motivation are the germinal forms of love and fear respectively. The sense of discomfort expressed in the call for the mother is implicitly the fear of isolation; and since isolation from the relationship which constitutes his existence, if it lasts too long, means death, it is implicitly the fear of death. The sense of comfort communicated by his expression of delight in being cared for is the germinal form of love. This bipolar, reciprocal, love and

fear motivation is concerned with maintaining the personal
relationship in a common life between mother and child. We
need draw attention only to two characteristics which have a
special importance for our further study. The first is that the
negative pole, in the child's behaviour as in the mother's,
falls within and is subordinated to the positive. Isolation from
the mother, if it becomes permanent, does involve death. The
baby who loses the mother loses his life. But the fear of isolation
functions in the child's life as a means of bringing the mother's
care into active operation and so eliminating the ground for
fear. It diversifies the child's experience of the relationship, and
institutes the rhythm of withdrawal and return to which I
referred in the first volume.[1] The second characteristic is this.
There is from the beginning an element of symbolic activity involved which has no organic or utilitarian purpose, and which
makes the relationship, as it were, an end in itself. The relationship is enjoyed, both by mother and child, for its own sake. The
mother not only does what is needful for the child: she fondles
him, caresses him, rocks him in her arms, and croons to him;
and the baby responds with expressions of delight in his mother's
care which have no biological significance. These gestures
symbolize a mutual delight in the relation which unites them in
a common life: they are expressions of affection through which
each communicates to the other their delight in the relationship,
and they represent, for its own sake, a consciousness of com-
municating. It is not long before the baby's cries convey, not
some organic distress, but simply the need for the mother's
presence to banish the sense of loneliness, and to reassure him of
her care for him. As soon as she appears, as soon as the baby is
in touch with her again, the crying ceases, and is replaced by a
smile of welcome.

[1] *The Self as Agent*, p. 181.

CHAPTER THREE

The Discrimination of the Other

We have determined the form of the original motivation of personal activity. We must complete this by considering the form of its development. For a person is an agent; consequently a static analysis provides at most the form of a starting-point, the zero of a developing series, which has full meaning only through the activity of which it is the origin. It will be desirable, therefore, to begin by reconsidering our conclusion from this point of view.

The starting-point of personal development, since a person is an agent, is the development of the ability to act. Action, we discovered,[1] is defined by intention, and so involves knowledge as a determinant of purposeful movement. But this presupposes its own negative, a motive consciousness which determines purposive behaviour without knowledge, as reaction to stimulus. Intention, therefore, presupposes motivation, and a complete account of action involves the consideration of its motivation as well as of its intention. Genetically, as we have seen, the negative is primary; and motivation is therefore prior in the temporal sequence of development to intention. For this reason, any understanding of personal development must begin with an attempt to formulate the pattern of personal motivation. This is one justification for concentrating attention at this point upon the development of motivation, to the exclusion of intention. The development of a person from infancy to maturity is a process of acquiring skills or, in other terms, of forming habits. This

---

[1] *The Self as Agent*, pp. 128, 172.

includes, of course, the development of the ability to form and to execute intentions. But these intentions are not fully serious; they have the character of play. The long-range intentions which affect a child's future are taken for him; and only when he 'comes of age' is he responsible, in the full sense, for his actions, and so master of his own intentions. If we consider the period of development to maturity as a whole, we must assign it a negative character, in the sense that the developing intentionality which it exhibits is itself subordinated and directed to the development of a system of motives, and so to the acquirement of a system of habits. This is the element of truth in Aristotle's doctrine of habituation.

We are justified, then, in considering the process of development as primarily concerned with motivation. There is, however, a further limitation which we shall set ourselves, if only to make the subject manageable within the limits of space at our disposal. We shall concentrate upon the positive personal aspect of the process, and neglect its negative component. This negative component is the organic aspect of personal life, which includes maturing and exercising the powers of the body, together with the developments of discriminating motive consciousness which are integrated with these. The child has to learn to discriminate and to co-ordinate the manifold of feeling, sense and muscular movement: he has to learn to stand, to walk, to feed himself, to put his clothes on, to speak, and in general to acquire and establish in himself the mechanisms of personal activity. The investigation of this development forms the subject-matter of child-psychology, and of the psychology of learning. For our philosophical purpose it is only necessary to recognize it and to presuppose it. This is not to minimize its importance in personal development, and we shall be compelled, in special contexts, to refer to it. But we are concerned with the positive aspect; with that which makes the development of the human being a personal, and not an organic development, and this, as we have seen, is to be found in the relation of persons to one another, of which the mother-child relation is the starting-point.

THE DISCRIMINATION OF THE OTHER

The positive aspect of personal development is therefore the development of this relation. Within this development of personal relationship the organic development functions as a differentiating element. Since persons are agents, their relations are realized in action; consequently the types of action in which the relationship is embodied must vary with the capacities for action of the persons concerned, though the personal motives of these varying actions may remain constant. The mother's love for the child is the constant motive of a varied set of activities which make up her care for him. These activities are differentiated by the variety of the child's organic needs and by the stage of his organic development. They are modified progressively by the variation in the child's capacity for action. The same obviously holds for the child's response to the mother's activity on his behalf. We ought, perhaps, to remind ourselves in this connection that the term 'organic', when applied to personal behaviour, does not refer to that which we have in common with the animals, though it includes whatever of this there may be. It refers to the habitual aspect of personal activity in abstraction from the intentionality to which it is normally subordinate.

With these explanations we may return to the starting-point of personal development in the original motivation-pattern of the infant's behaviour in relation to the mother. We have described it as a bipolar system, with positive and negative poles, each of which possesses an implicit reference to the personal Other. We have identified the positive pole with love and the negative with fear. This formal statement calls for explication and comment.

The original pattern of personal behaviour is not merely a starting-point. It is not left behind as the child grows up. It remains the ground pattern of all personal motivation at every stage of development. If the *terminus a quo* of the personal life is a helpless total dependence on the Other, the *terminus ad quem* is not independence, but a mutual interdependence of equals. In comparing human and animal development it is not enough to say that the human infant is dependent upon its parents for a much longer period. This tends to suggest that the difference is one of time; and that the child at length reaches the stage where he can provide for his own needs as an animal can from a much earlier age. But this is not the case. The boy who has reached maturity in dependence upon his parents does not then find himself fitted to wander off into the wilds and find food and shelter for himself in animal isolation. He finds employment in which he can earn money with which to buy what he needs. He exchanges a direct and personal dependence upon his family for a dependence on a wider society, a dependence which is impersonal and indirect. We can make the same point if we consider the behaviour to which the original pattern of motivation gives rise. This behaviour is, as we have seen,[1] a communication to another person, unconscious to start with on the infant's part, but understood and responded to by the adult. When we say then that the original motivation of personal behaviour remains as its ground pattern throughout life, we are merely insisting that communication is fundamental in all personal experience and determines its form. This includes the commonplaces that it is the power of speech which distinguishes us from the animals and that human life is inherently social. But it goes deeper than these, and both of them are somewhat superficial—and so misleading—observations. Speech is only one of the techniques of communication, however important, and it is not the earliest. It is an acquired skill. That man is social by nature is true, but highly ambiguous. Many animals are social; yet no species is social in the sense in which we are, for none has the form of its life determined from the beginning by communication. Communication is not the offspring of speech, but its parent.

We have identified the positive and negative poles of our personal motivation as 'love' and 'fear' respectively. This is necessary for identification, but it should be accompanied by a word of caution. Our language for the identification and discrimination of motives is both poor and imprecise. This is not

[1] See above, Chap. II, pp. 48 ff.

perhaps so great a defect as might appear at first sight. When we distinguish clearly between the motives and intentions of our actions, we find that our distinguishable motives are relatively few and extraordinarily persistent. The behaviour which they motivate, on the other hand, is highly complex and diversified. But this complexity arises chiefly from the fact that we act with knowledge, in terms of the world outside us, so that the form of our behaviour is determined by the variety and complexity of the situations in which we act. Moreover, we are normally unconscious of the motives of our actions, because our attention is focused upon the intention which determines them. It is only when action is thwarted or inhibited, when the motive is prevented from functioning in bodily movement, that it is reflected back upon itself, as it were, and so thrust into explicit consciousness as an emotion. So it comes about that we have occasion to speak of love and fear mainly in a complex situation where they force themselves with some violence upon our attention as emotions which disturb the normal attitudes and activities of our lives. This, no doubt, is why we tend to think of them as abnormal states of mind, and to contrast them with the cool 'unemotional' attitudes which we associate with 'rational' behaviour. This is a mistake; for a cool feeling is just as much a feeling as an excited one, and no activity, rational or irrational, practical or reflective, is possible in the absence of a motive. The reason why any strong emotional excitement tends to make us act wildly and 'irrationally' is not that emotion is 'irrational' or 'non-rational' but simply that by invading consciousness it distracts our attention from the situation in which we must act, and turns it inward upon our state of mind. Yet for this very reason it is easier to *identify* our motives when they are excited and so thrust upon our notice. When we identify the positive and negative poles of personal motivation as 'love' and 'fear' respectively, we are speaking of them not as perturbations of consciousness but as they function in behaviour to determine the direction in which we expend our energy.

But a further caution is necessary. We are speaking of love

and fear as personal motives, which must be distinguished from organic impulses. There are organic impulses to which the terms 'love' and 'fear' are frequently applied; erotic impulse in the former case and panic terror in the second. When 'love' is used to refer to sexual passion there is always, in my opinion, a confusion involved. For the motive of sexual behaviour is not necessarily 'love'; it may, for example, be revenge. But I need not press this, and we may treat it as a matter of linguistic usage. In the case of fear there is not a confusion in the use of terms, but a mere failure to distinguish between fear which is subject to intentional control, and the abnormal and rare experience of panic. What is decisive in this—as in the case of uncontrollable sexual impulse—is the complete loss of intentional control of behaviour, so that pure organic activity, pure reaction to stimulus, manifests itself. It may be important to remember both that this is possible and that it is highly exceptional.

When we identify the original motives of personal action with love and fear, the character which distinguishes them is the reference to a personal Other. The behaviour which they motivate is communication. It is only in this sense of the terms that they denote *personal* motives. The need which they express is one which can only be satisfied by another person's action. The behaviour which they motivate is therefore incomplete until it meets with a response from the other, and the character of the response—or indeed its occurrence—depends upon the other person. This primary and distinctive character of personal behaviour we shall refer to hereafter as the *mutuality* of the personal. It is what we mean when we say that the personal is constituted by the relation of persons. The reference to the personal Other is constitutive for all personal existence.

The reference to the other person differs in positive and negative motivation. In the former case it is direct: in the latter, indirect. Love is love for the other, fear is fear for oneself. But this fear for oneself refers to the behaviour of the other. Since mutuality is constitutive for the personal, it follows that 'I' need 'you' in order to be myself. My primary fear is, therefore, that 'you' will not respond to my need, and that in consequence my personal existence will be frustrated. Fear, as a personal motive, is at once fear of the other and fear for oneself. Thus both love and fear fall within the personal relation; both refer to this relation; and fear, as the negative, presupposes love and is subordinate to it.

To complete this statement we must notice that both the positive and the negative motives are operative in all personal action. It is for this reason that we have described the original motivation of the personal as bipolar, and 'love' and 'fear' as the positive and negative poles of a single motivation. This accords with the form of the personal as we have determined it —a positive which contains, is constituted by and subordinates its own negative. It is easy to see that this must be so. Action contains two elements—or, as we phrased it, has two dimensions —movement and knowledge. Consequently, it is deliberate, while a reaction to stimulus is impulsive. The motivation of action, therefore, must contain an inhibiting element which prevents the immediate habitual response, provides a counter-acting impulse to reflection, and allows the apprehension of the situation to determine what we do. Fear is in its nature in-hibitory; and the most positive action must contain an element of negative motivation, if it is not to be completely thoughtless and reckless. The most pervasive expression of this is the con-tinual presence in action of an awareness—even if it is normally implicit—of the possibility of making a mistake, of doing the wrong thing. The operation of choice between alternative possibilities is thus necessarily the effect of a negative motiva-tion. In the original 'You and I' situation, it represents the fact that the fulfilment of my purpose depends not merely upon me, but also upon you; so that there is always present the possibility that my call for help may not meet with a response. 'My' success depends upon 'your' motive and 'your' intention.

In the alternative case, no action can be motived purely by fear. For a totally negative motivation would inhibit action totally. We should be 'paralysed by fear'. The presence of an element of positive motivation is necessary if there is to be a deliberate action to deal with the danger that is apprehended. To express this character of personal behaviour we must agree upon a terminology which will refer to it as accurately as possible. We shall adopt the following terminology. We shall say that personal motivation is bipolar, having positive and negative poles which we identify by reference to 'love' and 'fear' respectively. We shall then distinguish between action which is positively and action which is negatively motived by saying that in the former case the positive pole is dominant and subordinates the negative; while in the latter the positive is subordinated to the dominant negative. We shall express the function of the subordinated pole by saying that it works as a discriminating force, that is to say, it makes possible a discriminating activity. And having used the emotions of love and fear to identify the positive and negative poles of personal motivation, we can speak in the future of positive and negative motives simply, using the terms 'love' and 'fear' only where a more specific identification is desirable.

There is one other matter of terminology, closely related to what we have discussed, which it may be as well to refer to now. Action which is negatively motived is defensive. Fear, as we have said, is for oneself, and the agent himself is the centre of reference for the action. We may find this mode of distinction a useful one; and we shall refer to it by saying that negatively motived action is 'egocentric', while positively motived action, which has its centre of reference outside oneself, in the Other, we shall describe as 'heterocentric'. This distinction between egocentric and heterocentric action becomes paramount when we consider the subordination of motive to intention. The mother's care for the child, for example, necessarily includes a negative element—an anxiety lest her child should damage itself or get hurt. If the child's clothes were to catch fire, the mother would take immediate action to extinguish the flames, and her action would be accompanied by a feeling of fear and anxiety, perhaps of extreme terror. But her action is not therefore negatively motived. For it is clearly heterocentric, at least under normal conditions. Her fear is not for herself, but for the child, and she may act in a fashion which recklessly disregards her own safety. Her action indeed would be recognized as a signal expression of her love for the child, in spite of or indeed because of the extremity of fear which she experiences. We recognize at once that the fear is itself an expression of her love of the child, that it is the negative and subordinate component in a persistently positive motivation, called into prominence in consciousness by the character of a particular situation. This fact that the emotion felt by an agent at the moment of action is not necessarily the motive of his action, is one of the main reasons why we are so apt to be mistaken about our motives, while the judgment of others is often more correct than our own. For others must judge our motives from the character of our behaviour, while we ourselves tend to judge them by the feelings of which we are conscious. These are no doubt components of our motivation; but they are not necessarily, or even normally, its defining characters. For what determines the presence of a particular emotion in the form of consciousness is the character of the situation upon which our attention is directed. We may even go farther and say that the emotion felt is unlikely to reveal the true character of the motive. For one of the major conditions of the invasion of consciousness by a particular emotion is its inhibition as a motive of action. The mother's felt terror when the child's clothes catch fire is occasioned by the fact that she must act in a way that disregards her own safety. Her natural fear for herself must be inhibited as motive; consequently it is prevented from expressing itself in action and reflected back into an 'internal' effect, which is the *feeling* of fear as a strong emotion. It is the absence of fear from the action that explains its intrusive appearance in consciousness. The resulting ambiguity provides one reason for avoiding the terms 'love' and 'fear' in discussing motivation, except for purposes of identification.

We are now ready to discuss the development of this original motivation, though since our purpose is formal our only concern is to disengage its persistent pattern from the endless complexities of the actual process of growth. The first point that claims our attention is the derivation of a third original motive from the interrelation of the positive and negative motives in the personal situation. As we have identified the first two by reference to the emotions of love and fear, we can identify the third by reference to hatred, but with the same caution. In some respects it might be better to use the term 'resentment' instead of 'hatred'; though in that case we should have to replace 'fear' by 'anxiety', and 'love' by 'caring'—since the term 'charity', which would be the corresponding word, has been debased in usage. I call this motive original because, like love and fear, it is a universal component in the relation of persons, inherent in the personal situation in all its forms. I call it derivative because it presupposes love and fear as operative motives. It originates in the frustration of love by fear, through the mutuality of the personal relation. The behaviour which expresses love requires, for its completion, a response from the other to whom it is directed. Love is fulfilled only when it is reciprocated. If the response is refused, the action which expresses the positive motive is frustrated. Now, in general, the personal relation is unavoidable, since the personal is constituted by the personal relation; and the refusal of mutuality is the frustration of personal existence absolutely. This can be seen in the original mother-child relation in its stark simplicity. If the mother refuses to care for the child, the child must die. But when a rejected lover commits suicide the motivation is the same. The act is irrational because there are other alternatives open for the fulfilment of his personal life. In general, however, and in principle, the 'You and I' relation which makes us persons is such that if you act positively to me, so offering to enter into friendly relations, and I reject your advance, I threaten your existence as a person in an absolute fashion. I throw you back on yourself, and the negative pole of your motivation must become dominant. You are afraid for your own personal existence, which is threatened by my motivation in relation with you. Consequently you necessarily resent my action; and if the relation is unavoidable then your resentment becomes hatred—a persistent motive in your personal relation to me; not, of course, we must remember, a persistent *emotion* which you feel towards me. Hatred, therefore, as an original motive is inevitable in all personal relations, though, like the other motives, only as a component of a complex motivation, not necessarily dominant, and subject to the control of intention. It is inevitable, because it is impossible that you should always be able to respond to me in the way that my action expects. This is why forbearance and forgiveness are necessities of positive personal relationship. The rejection of personal relationship itself is a negative aspect of personal relationship, and itself enforces a reciprocity of negation. In so far as I threaten your personal fulfilment you can only reciprocate by threatening mine. Hatred, therefore, is the emotion by which we can identify the motive of mutual negation in the personal relation. If it completely escapes from intentional control it issues in murder. For this reason we contrast love and hatred as opposites rather than love and fear. Both have a direct reference to the Other. They sustain a positive and a negative relation of persons respectively. Yet the opposition of love and fear as contraries is more fundamental. For a negative relation of persons is a practical contradiction. It is a relation which is at once maintained and refused, and which is therefore inherently self-stultifying. It can only be maintained by a positive motive: its rejection can only mean that this positive motive is continuously inhibited by a negative one. Now we have seen that a positive relation of persons must contain and subordinate a negative element: the possibility of a negative relation can only signify an inversion of this motivation in which the negative element is dominant and subordinates the positive. Hatred, therefore, is a motive of self-frustration. Since the 'You and I' relation constitutes both the 'You' and the 'I' persons, the relation to the 'You' is necessary for my personal existence. If, through fear of the 'You', I reject this relation, I frustrate my own being. It follows that hatred cannot, as a motive of action, be universalized. It presupposes both love and fear, and if it could be total it would destroy the possibility of personal existence. It is no doubt this that underlies, even if it does not completely justify, our tendency to assume that suicide is evidence of mental derangement.

This mutuality of hatred as the motive of a negative relation of persons is clearly an evil. Hatred itself, as an original and necessary motive in the constitution of the personal, is perhaps what is referred to by theology as original sin. At any rate, the distinction we have just drawn between a positive and a negative relation of persons is the origin of the distinction between good and evil. But this is a subject which will claim our attention later. I have introduced it here because it has a direct bearing upon the pattern of personal development, which we are seeking to formulate.

The first aspect of this development which we must notice might be described as the differentiation of the Other. We have seen that in the relation of mother and child the term 'mother' has not an organic, but a personal denotation. It refers to the adult person who cares for the baby. But only in very abnormal circumstances can this be a single person. Most of the mothering of the baby will normally be undertaken by one adult and usually it will be its female parent. But it will be shared, to a greater or less extent, by others; by a father, a grandmother, an aunt, an elder sister or brother, a nurse or a neighbour. Now there is no ground for thinking that in the very earliest weeks of his life the infant is able to discriminate between the different persons, or indeed to recognize objects at all, and certainly not by sight. The primary perception of the Other, we have seen, is tactual. The correlation of sight and touch has to be learned. Consequently, the primary perception of the Other must arise from the discrimination between being tactually cared for and the absence of this; and this discrimination cannot serve to distinguish different Others. Since the infant's motivation contains an implicit reference to the Other, the recognition of the Other as 'What responds to my cry' must become explicit so soon as any power of discrimination is acquired. And since this is the first cognition, we can understand why 'all cognition is recognition'. It is the repeated process of crying for the mother and being handled by the mother in response that elicits the recognition, and with it both memory and expectation. This recognition is at once the dawn of knowledge, the awareness that something has been going on which has only now been noticed, and the expectation of its continuance. And what has been happening is a rhythm of withdrawal and return in the tactual contact of mother and child. The language in which this has to be described is by far too definite and explicit, since language arises in and is adapted to a much more definite and discriminated level of personal experience, and it must be interpreted accordingly. The central point is this, that so soon as the infant can perceive at all its perception is a perception of the Other and therefore knowledge, however minimal. There is no problem of how an originally subjective experience becomes objective. If there were it would be insoluble. The idea that there is such a problem arises from the assumption that language is essential to knowledge. What is essential to knowledge is *communication*, of which language is the most important but not the only medium. The original adaptation of the human being to life contains the reference to the Other, and his first behaviour is an unconscious communication. Communication is for all human beings a fact before it becomes an act, before explicit perception and the formation of an intention is possible for us. The reference to the Other, of which the objectivity of thought is a particular case, is present from the beginning.

The first knowledge, then, is knowledge of the personal Other —the Other with whom I am in communication, who responds to my cry and cares for me. This is the starting-point of all knowledge and is presupposed at every stage of its subsequent development. Consequently there is no problem about our knowledge of other persons. On the contrary, any philosophy which finds itself required by its own logic to ask the question

'How do we know that there are other persons?' has refuted itself by a *reductio ad absurdum*, and should at once revise its original assumptions. For any assertion—not to speak of any effort of proof—presupposes this knowledge by the mere fact that it is a communication. If we did not know that there are other persons we could know literally nothing, not even that we ourselves existed. To be a person is to be in communication with the Other. The knowledge of the Other is the absolute presupposition of all knowledge, and as such is necessarily indemonstrable.

But this original knowledge of the Other, as the correlate of my own activity, is undiscriminated. The development of knowledge is its discrimination. We are discussing here, of course, primary knowledge, knowledge as a dimension of action, not a reflective activity which intends the improvement of knowledge. We found in our first volume that the primary certainty was the 'I do'. But we were then talking abstractly, from the point of view of the solitary self withdrawn into itself in reflection. We now see how this must be completed in the concrete. The 'I do' is the correlate of 'the Other does', and since knowledge is primarily 'of the Other', the 'I do' now appears as the negative which falls within the knowledge of the Other as agent, and is necessary to it. In the actual situation in which we all begin our individual existence—in the mother-child relation—our own agency is negative. It is the Other who does everything for us, who is the Agent upon whose action we are totally dependent, and within whose activity, supporting and limiting us, our own action is progressively achieved. If we use, as we must, the reflective language of maturity, we may say that the first knowledge is the recognition of the Other as the person or agent in whom we live and move and have our being.

My first discrimination of the Other is into a number of different persons all of whom are in communication with me and with one another. The Other acquires the character of a community of which I am a member. The details of this process do not concern us. We may leave them to the psychologist. We need only notice a few formal points. The gradual enlargement of the group of persons to which we stand in relation and with whom we are in communication is a commonplace in all studies of the process of human development from infancy. It runs from the family circle, which is the first community and the model for all other communities, to the vision of a community of all persons. Our interest centres in the universal pattern which it exhibits. In thinking of this we must remember that the discrimination of the Other is a practical, not a reflective discrimination. It is a discrimination in behaviour in relation to the Other. The ability to distinguish different members of the family to which the child belongs is established very early and manifests itself in differences of behaviour in relation with each. It is acquired long before speech, and, at least in rudimentary form, before any efficient correlation of hand and eye.

This differentiation of behaviour in relation to different persons involves a complication of the system of motivation. For the child may be negatively motived towards one and positively to another, and the intensity of these motivations, whether positive or negative, will vary with the extent and frequency with which the other person cares for him. The mother will remain the central figure and the others will be subsidiary figures, related to the child through their relation to her. New and more complex motives develop, of which jealousy is possibly the most important. These secondary complexes of motivation depend upon the discrimination of the Other as a group of persons in personal relation to one another and in personal relation, as a group and as individuals, to myself. Their reference to the Other is therefore to a community, and they are either positive or negative. In either case their objective is the unity of the Other. The group has a personal centre. In the original community the mother is this personal centre. She is, as it were, the personal unity of the persons composing the community, since she cares for them all and all need her love. Each is personally related to all the others by this personal relation to the central figure which is common to them all. For each the maintenance of the positive relation to the mother depends upon maintaining the unity of the Other. But this may be sought either positively or negatively; either by the inclusion of the subordinate others in the positive relation to the mother, or in their exclusion from it. This negative motive appears emotionally as jealousy. In its original form it is the motive of the childish refusal to share the mother's care and affection with others. Formally, it is a regressive effort to restore the unity of the Other in its original undifferentiated form.

The pattern of this aspect of personal development is now before us, so far as it concerns the differentiation of the personal Other. But before summing it up we must refer to another aspect of the process—the differentiation between persons and non-persons or things. The recognition of the distinction between persons and things comes considerably later than the differentiation of persons, and is not definitely established for some years after the child has learned to speak. Like primitive man, young children are animists; and to overcome animism require a considerable experience, and some capacity for abstract thought. It is very difficult for us to recognize this, and still more difficult to realize effectively the philosophical consequences.

Primitive animism, whether in the race or in the individual, shows genetically what we have already discovered analytically[1] —that the concept of a material world is abstract and derivative. The material is, in fact, the non-personal; and as a negative conception, it depends for its definition upon the positive which it negates. Our knowledge of the material presupposes, both logically and genetically, a knowledge of the personal. Logically, the Other is the correlate of the Self as Agent. It is that which resists, and in resisting supports, my intention. Since Self and Other are primary correlates, any determination of one of them must formally characterize the other also. The form of the Self and the form of the Other must be identical: the categories through which both are thought must be the same. If I am the agent, then the Other is the other agent. If my act is the realization of my intention, then the activity of the Other is the realiza-

[1] *The Self as Agent*, p. 173.

tion of his intention. Thus the primary correlation, on which all knowledge rests, is the 'You and I' in active relation. How then is it possible for the Other to be known as non-personal? Only by a *reduction of the concept of the Other which excludes part of its definition*; only, that is to say, by a partial negation: only by down-grading the 'You' in the 'You and I' to the status of 'It'. If we do this, however, we necessarily reduce its correlate, the 'I' in the same fashion. The non-personal Other is thus the correlate of the Self as body, that is, as a material object. Now what is excluded in this abstraction is intention. The non-personal Other is that which is active without intention. Its correlate is myself unintentionally active. For this reason I remarked earlier[1] that we should not know what was meant by a body falling freely through space if we had never fallen downstairs.

Genetically, the first correlate of the Self is the mother; and this personal Other, as we have seen, is gradually differentiated in experience till it becomes the whole community of persons of which I am an individual member. Side by side with this differentiation, but dependent on it, and falling within it, there develops the negative differentiation between personal and non-personal elements in the Other. The distinction between persons and things is no doubt implicit in the distinction of two or more persons, since this distinction itself is made against a background. Once we have become used to apprehending 'things' it is difficult for us to conceive a condition in which the distinction is not obvious. We tend, indeed, to reverse the process, and to consider any personal apprehension of the material world—in poetic imagination, for instance, or in primitive nature-worship —as a personification of what is known, in unexcited observation, as inanimate. Genetically, however, we arrive at the inanimate object through a process of depersonalization. It is here specially important to remember that it is not the visual, but the tactual perception of the Other that is primary, and that what is discriminated is not simply what is there, but depends upon interest, upon the selective activity of attention in

---

[1] *The Self as Agent*, p. 117.

the service of purposes. The original discrimination is simply the focusing of attention. For the infant it is that which responds to his cry. When he comes to discriminate more than one person in the Other, it is at first as two centres of response. Whatever else he distinguishes is not an individual in its own right, but a concomitant, related more or less closely to this focus of interest. It is the whole Other that is personal. When two foci are established, the problem set him is to divide the whole Other into two referring some of it to the one and some to the other centre. With this comes the further problem of referring some to myself as 'mine', and some to the others as 'his' or 'hers'. Indeed, this problem remains always incompletely solved. 'My body' continues to occupy an ambiguous position in relation to me. From one point of view it *is* me or part of me; from another it is an object which I 'have' or 'own' or 'possess', as I possess my clothes or my fountain-pen. For the small child this ambiguity occurs with all objects. They all 'belong' to somebody and are identified with their owner, and, indeed, nearly all the objects of his environment are artifacts, and are private property. The growing child discovers early that everything, including his brothers and sisters, himself, and even his mother, 'belong' to father.

It must then be a considerable feat of young intelligence to consider a material object out of relation to persons, and so as belonging to itself, and having a being of its own. How this is actually achieved, and by what stages, it is for the psychologist to tell us. A summary statement is sufficient for our purpose. The non-personal is discriminated within the unity of the personal as a negative. It is that in the Other which does not respond to my call. If I am to enter into active relation with it then I must go to it; it will not come to me. The relation I have with it lacks the mutuality of a personal relation. It is, then, that which can be moved, but which cannot move itself. Secondly, it is that which corresponds in the Other to myself when I am moved but do not move myself—when I fall if my support is removed, when my movements are not under my control and so are unintentional; or when some other person lifts me and carries me from one place to another. It is that which in action is passive to action. It resists me, and so is other than me; but its resistance is a passive resistance. Its movements must be referred to something other than itself. Thirdly, and following from these, it is that which, in the largest sense, is a means to action. It is, for example, an instrument or tool, like the poker with which we stir the fire: it is stuff which can be formed or shaped, like cloth from which clothes are made or the plasticine I play with. It is the material I use to satisfy my organic needs—the food I eat or the materials which mother mixes up together to make my birthday cake. In general, the non-personal is that which, in action, is always means and never agent.

Some non-personal elements in the Other are depersonalized with greater difficulty than others. They are, on the one hand, those which are too big or too distant for us to use, the earth, the sky, the sea, the sun, moon and stars are examples. The easiest to depersonalize are small objects, mostly artifacts, which are in familiar use by different members of the family group and are not specially associated with one or other as 'his own'. On the other hand, the depersonalizing becomes more difficult the more a material object is the exclusive property of a particular person. For then they tend to characterize him, and to present themselves as expressions or even as attributes of his individual existence. It is this difficulty which is, as I have mentioned already, at its maximum in the case of a person's body, so that a complete depersonalization is practically impossible, and an insuperable ambiguity remains.

Yet even with regard to common objects which we all easily depersonalize, and dissociate from the personal Other as inanimate things, the ambiguity lurks in the background, and re-emerges in our reflective activities. We need not here refer especially to those mystical or quasi-mystical experiences which visit some people frequently and others rarely, if at all. For these, if they stood alone, might well be dismissed as regressions to an infantile state of consciousness. What is more impressive is the development of physical science. For the *modus operandi* of depersonalization is largely visual; and the visible individuality of macroscopic objects plays a leading role in the process. But it is just this individuality—this 'being-for-itself'—that is dissolved by scientific reflection. All objects alike become temporary specifications of a universal 'stuff' or 'matter'. The search for a real individual—for an existing unit of the non-personal—leads to the atom; and all material objects become congregations of identical units in the void. Presently the atom dissolves in its turn; and in the process energy takes precedence of matter or body, just as in our present philosophical effort to understand the personal, action takes precedence of object. The non-personal becomes a vast multiplicity of somewhat imprecisely located centres for the reception, storage and transmission of energy. And what is energy? It is action without an agent. Is this really thinkable? Only, it would seem, in terms of those automatic activities of our own for which we disclaim all personal responsibility. They are and yet they are not our own. In terms of the form of the personal they are negatively personal; instances of the negative which is necessary to the constitution of the personal. So we saddle our bodies with the responsibility that we disown.

In discussing the depersonalization of the personal Other as the formation of a notion of the material existent, we have omitted all reference to the organic. This has been a deliberate omission. For genetically, the organic world remains persistently ambiguous, and the contrast of personal and non-personal is a contrast between persons and things. For this reason reflective thought tends to operate within a dualist framework, classifying all possible entities or events as either material or mental; and classifying philosophies as either idealist or realist, mentalist or materialist. So when we isolate the organic for reflective understanding we seek to understand it either through categories drawn from the personal or from the material field. The controversy in biology between vitalists and mechanists is a very recent memory, and the temporary victory for the chemists is not likely to prove decisive. Organic chemistry can hardly hope to cover the whole field of biological enquiry, since it must abjure any form of representation which has even a quasi-teleological flavour.

I do not propose to remedy this omission, since to do so would add little to our own purpose. We need only notice that the ambiguity lies in our relation, as persons, to the world of organic life. It is our practical relation that draws the primary distinctions, and from this point of view the facts themselves are ambiguous. For the growing child there are some animals, and even some plants in the garden, which are, as it were, parts of the family circle, which belong to people and are fed and housed and cared for. There are others which are simply articles of diet, like fish or carrots, which we make part of ourselves by devouring them. From another point of view, there are animals which are kept as pets. The family dog will respond to the child's call by coming to him; and will reply to expressions of affection with expressions of pleasure. The fancy that makes the big dog the children's nurse in *Peter Pan* has its roots in reality and requires no violent effort of imagination—only a gentle stretching. Yet it can only apply to a very few of the highest forms of animal life: and even so it crosses the absolute dividing line. This is not so much due to the absence of speech, as to the inability of even even the highest organism to care for us, even for a child, in the practical ways in which we must be cared for if we are to survive and mature as persons.

In short, and to conclude, the discrimination of the Other into persons, organisms and material objects is primarily practical. We have to learn three different modes of action in relation to three different types of Other. The mode of behaviour which is appropriate to persons is inappropriate in our dealings with things; while the mode that is right in our relations with organisms stands midway between the other two, holding out a hand to either. But if we try to make these distinctions absolute, for purposes of reflection, in definitive concepts, the unity of the Other as one world in which all are related infects our efforts with ambiguity which we cannot resolve, and which tempts us to reduce two of them to the third. But though we may satisfy our craving for theoretical simplicity in this ingenious fashion, the moment we act the distinctions reassert themselves inescapably.

CHAPTER FOUR

The Rhythm of Withdrawal and Return

We considered, in the last chapter, that aspect of personal development which concerns the differentiation of the original personal Other into a world of persons, organisms and material objects united by their relations to one another. This is, of course, the formal development of our primary *knowledge*. To consider it first has methodological advantages, but it is not without its dangers. For it may lead us back insensibly to that dualism of subject and object from which we are seeking to escape. It seems to presuppose an observer self standing over against the Other and gradually differentiating the Object with increasing distinctness and clarity. We have, therefore, to remind ourselves now that knowledge is the negative dimension of action, and that a self is primarily agent, and as such in active relation with the Other of which he forms part. Even if we confine our attention to the development of cognition in the child, we have to remember the mutuality of the personal relation which determines its form. Self and Other are correlatives, and the discrimination of the one involves a correlative discrimination of the other. If within the unity of the Other I discriminate personal, organic and material aspects, I discriminate these same aspects in myself. Moreover, in discriminating myself from the Other, it is always as belonging to the Other. The philosophical difficulty here we may leave unexplored until we come to discuss self-consciousness at a later stage.

We must now, however, turn our attention to the positive

aspect of our personal development, that is to say to the development of the person as an agent, of which the development of the capacity to discriminate the Other is merely the negative aspect. We must consider the form of the development of the original system of motivation. For this purpose we must return to our starting-point in the relation of mother and child. We have noticed[1] how the periodic repetition of the normal acts of mothering—feeding, washing and so forth—sets up a rhythm of withdrawal and return within the relation. As the infant's capacity for awareness increases, this rhythmic recurrence of the mother's attentions will, we must presume, establish itself in the child's consciousness as expectation based upon memory, and so provide the beginnings of knowledge. We are justified in using the term knowledge at this early stage, because the reference to the Other is, as we have seen, implicit from the beginning, and must become explicit so soon as the necessary skills in discriminating and correlating sensory and motor experiences are present. The remembered response of the mother to his cries is expected to repeat itself at regular intervals. Now this involves a number of fundamental lessons to be learned. The first is learning to wait for the response to his appeal. The second is learning to know the Other as the repetition of the same, a lesson which underlies all recognition of order and form. This is the reason why a regular and invariant routine in the care of the young is of such importance; and it is the source of the child's demand for an invariant repetition of what he is familiar with in a story or a game.

But this learning to wait and to expect has an even more fundamental bearing upon the development of motivation. The child's recognition of a need for the mother to do something for him is negatively motived. The persistence of this need, since he can do nothing for its satisfaction, is accompanied by a growing discomfort and anxiety. Learning to wait for the right time involves, therefore, the subordination of this negative motive to a positive attitude of confidence that the expected response will

[1] *Supra*, Chap. III, p. 76.

come in due time. This trust in the Other does not dispose of the discomfort or the need. The negative motive remains operative; but the sting is taken out of it by its integration in a complex attitude that is, as a whole, positively determined. The expectation of the coming satisfaction can indeed be enjoyed, as men deliberately undertake and enjoy the dangers and labours and discomforts of climbing Mount Everest, in the expectation of achievement. So the infant's expectation is grounded in imagination; and his waiting is filled with the symbolic satisfaction of his desire in phantasy; the images he forms and the feelings of anticipatory pleasure which accompany them persist through the period of waiting, and coalesce, as it were, with the actual satisfaction when it comes. This exercising of the power of phantasy is the first stage in the development of reflection, and the succession of anticipation and satisfaction—with the same images accompanying both—institutes the primary distinction between imagining and perceiving.

But this state of positive motivation differentiated by the negative motive it contains and dominates depends upon the constant fulfilment of the expectation at the proper time. The expectation is, in fact, a prediction based on experience and constantly verified. But the unexpected may happen; the prediction may not be verified. Then the basis of confidence and security is broken. If the response to his cry is too long delayed, or if the mother's effort to relieve his distress is unsuccessful, then the negative motive is no longer subordinated to a positive, confident expectation. It becomes dominant, and finds expression in a paroxysm of rage and terror, and what power of phantasy the child has acquired will lend itself to the symbolic representation of danger.

In the earliest stage of our life this reversal of the natural dominance of the positive motive is occasional and accidental. It foreshadows however a periodic reversal which is necessary and inevitable in passing from one stage to the next. If a child is to grow up, he must learn, stage by stage, to do for himself what has up to that time been done for him by the mother. But at all the crucial points, at least, the decision rests with the mother, and therefore it must take the form of a deliberate refusal on her part to continue to show the child those expressions of her care for him that he expects. This refusal is, of course, itself an expression of the mother's care for him. But the child's stock of knowledge is too exiguous, the span of his anticipation too short, for him to understand this. For him, the refusal can only mean the breakdown of the relationship by which and in which he has his being. In his need he calls to the Other, but the Other is deaf to his entreaty. He is thrown back upon himself. His world has collapsed into irrationality; for the order in his experience of the Other is recurrence without change, the continuous repetition of identity. The constants of his experience of the world have disappeared; his anticipations have not been verified. His predictions are still, as it were, dogmas; he has not yet learned to treat them as hypotheses. The formula of his confidence is 'this or nothing'. So he faces what is for him the ultimate threat to his existence—isolation from the Other by the act of the Other.

The necessary consequence of such a situation is that the motivation system of the child's behaviour is thrown into reverse. The negative pole becomes dominant. Activity becomes egocentric, concerned with the defence of himself in a world which is indifferent to his needs, a world which acts in mysterious ways of its own, paying no attention to his desires. The emotional tone of such a phase of experience is one of anxiety; a general anxiety which, if it were to become permanent, must pass into despair. It is, of course, mitigated and qualified in various ways. For the positive motives remain active, though in subordination, differentiating the behaviour, and instigating an effort to overcome the negation and to restore the normal dominance of the positive. One aspect of this is that there is a positive pleasure for the child in acquiring and exercising the skill to do for himself what the mother refuses any longer to do for him. But it is important to recognize that this and other mitigating factors cannot of themselves provide a solution; that there is in fact no way in which the child can save himself from the anxiety which besets him. For the problem concerns the personal relation between himself and his mother: the anxiety is the fear that his mother does not love him any more, and he depends upon the mother while she does not depend upon him, at least in the same sense. He must indeed make an effort if there is to be a restoration of the mutual confidence that has been broken; but this can only succeed through the action of the mother. For since it was by his mother's action that the child's confidence was broken, it is only by her action that this confidence can be restored. If we may use the language of mature human reflection which, though its content is much richer, has an identical form, the child can only be rescued from his despair by the grace of the mother; by a revelation of her continued love and care which convinces him that his fears are groundless.

In this fashion there is established that rhythm of withdrawal and return which constitutes the universal and necessary pattern of personal development. Our immediate interest lies in its empirical functioning in the child's growth to maturity. But its importance is so great that we should first consider the pattern in its universal aspect, as a pure and necessary form. To do this we must consider the complete cycle, from the positive through the negative back to the positive, as ideally complete. This perfect achievement of the transition is, as we shall see, hardly to be expected in empirical experience. The overcoming of the negative always remains problematical.

The rhythm of withdrawal and return is the full dynamic expression of the form of the personal, as a positive which includes, is constituted by and subordinates its own negative. It is a succession of positive and negative phases which, taken together, constitute the unity of a personal experience. The negative phase, therefore, depends upon, and is subordinate to, the positive, and the whole activity can only be defined through the positive. The negative, as we have seen, has meaning only by reference to the positive, and is therefore, as a phase of activity, for the sake of the positive. The withdrawal is for the sake of the return; and its necessity lies in this, that it differentiates the positive phase by enriching its content. Without the negative there could be no development of the positive, but only the repetition *ad infinitum* of an original undifferentiated identity.

Now the original unity which is developed in this way is a relation of persons. It is the unity of a common life. The 'You and I' relation, we must recall, constitutes the personal, and both the 'You' and the 'I' are constituted, as individual persons, by the mutuality of their relation. Consequently, the development of the individual person is the development of his relation to the Other. Personal individuality is not an original given fact. It is achieved through the progressive differentiation of the original unity of the 'You and I'. If this sounds difficult or paradoxical, it is yet a commonplace in some of its manifestations. We all distinguish ourselves, as individuals, from the society of which we are members and to which we belong. The paradox is the same: for we at once assert ourselves as constituent members of the society while opposing it to ourselves as the 'other-than-I'. So the child discovers himself as an individual by contrasting himself, and indeed by wilfully opposing himself to the family *to which he belongs*; and this *discovery* of his individuality is at the same time the *realization* of his individuality. We are part of that from which we distinguish ourselves and to which, as agents, we oppose ourselves. In this—which is, indeed, simply another manifestation of the form of the personal—we may find the answer to many of the questions which puzzle the moralist; the existence of conscience, for example, of responsibility and the moral struggle; or, more generally, of the capacity which is possessed by a person, and only by a person, to represent his fellows—to feel and think and act, not for himself but for the other.

The difficulty we feel arises mainly because we are accustomed to think from the standpoint of reflection, and not of action. Persons are agents; and the relation of persons is a relation of agents, and in general is a *conditio sine quâ non* of action. Without the support of a resistance there can be no action; and the resistance must, as we recognized,[1] be the resis-

---

[1] *The Self as Agent*, p. 145.

tance of a personal Other. Consequently, both the relation itself and the rhythm of its development are not merely matter of fact, though necessarily including matter of fact. They are matter of intention. Thus the negative phase, just as much as the positive, falls within the relation and presupposes it even while negating it. My withdrawal from the Other is itself a phase of my relation to the Other. The isolation of the self does not annul the relation; but refuses it. And since the relation is practical—since it is a relation of agents—the refusal is a practical activity which *intends* the annulment of the relation which it presupposes. There is here a radical contradiction in action. Since any personal relation enters into the constitution of the persons whom it relates, to annul the relation is to annul oneself, and to achieve the intention could only mean to destroy oneself along with the other. But further, the relation itself is not mere matter of fact, but matter of intention. To annul it, therefore, must mean not merely to bring it to an end as matter of fact; it must mean to annul the intention, and therefore the action, which constitutes it. Now time is the form of action, and consequently to annul the action implies a reversal of the past. But this is impossible. The most we can do is, as we sometimes say, to make it *as if* it had never been. The most that such negative relation in action can achieve is a *symbolic* annulment; the appearance but not the reality of annulment.

Consider, as an example, the following situation. An only son has publicly disgraced his family. His father, bitterly affected by the disgrace, decides that he will have no more to do with the fellow and publicly disowns him. He disinherits his son, erases his name from the family record, refuses to see him, and cuts him 'dead' if he meets him by accident. If anyone refers to his son in his presence, he replies with a stony emphasis, 'I have no son.' In such a case the relation of father and son remains a fact, and the father is perfectly aware of this. Indeed, his behaviour presupposes the fact. He insists he has no son because he knows, and the people to whom he speaks also know, and know that he knows that he has. The non-existence of his son is thus not matter of fact, but matter of intention; but this intention is unrealizable, since it could only be realized by altering the past. It is not sufficient to say that he wishes his son were dead; it would be truer to say that he wishes his son had never been born. But even this is not a satisfactory diagnosis, for a wish is not an intention, and he behaves deliberately as though the facts were other than they are. He might, of course, kill his son, but that would be no solution. For what he intends to annul is not his son's future, and not merely his son's past, but his own past in having a son and caring for him. His behaviour can only be symbolic. Even if he were to kill his son and then himself, his action would be merely symbolic. It would symbolize, in a particular case, what is here asserted as a general principle, that the positive personal relation with his son is for him the sole intrinsic good, so that when this is negated in intention, it becomes impossible for him to intend his own existence, or that of his son.

There is always an element of illusion associated with the negative phase in the rhythm of personal development. This, indeed, is one aspect of its negativity. In the case of the child whose mother refuses to satisfy his expectation any longer, it *appears* that she refuses any longer to care for him; yet in reality her refusal is itself an expression of her continuing care for him. The illusion is necessary. The refusal throws his world into chaos. For it is the household routine, not the orderly succession of the seasons, which guarantees for the child the 'uniformity of nature'. The failure of the repetition of the same in his mother's care for him is to him what the failure of the sun to rise in due course would be for us. For him as for us, the possibility of life depends upon the faith that the future will be as the past, that we have a right to believe in the fulfilment of expectations based upon past experience. But expectation is relative to experience. We have learned that the constants we have found in experience may not represent the structure of reality in general; but hold only within a limited range of experience, as special cases of wider constancies. We have learned that the order of the world is more complex than our knowledge of it had led us to believe.

We have learned, in science, that all our generalizations are hypothetical, that our best grounded predictions are provisional; we have even learned to see the search for the falsification of our expectations as the surest path to a wider knowledge of the world. The child is only beginning to learn this; and what he is learning is the distinction between appearance and reality. It is necessary that the mother should refuse him what he has every reason to expect; it is necessary that within the relationship with her he should be forced into negativity, believe that she has ceased to care for him and be afraid. For only so can he experience the distinction between positive and negative in its fundamental manifestations; as the distinction between real and unreal, between good and evil, beautiful and ugly, true and false. For all of us, at any stage, development depends upon the rhythm of withdrawal and return; and this is true for societies as for individuals. If the rhythm ceases, development ceases with it, and we are ripe for death or for destruction.

This will become clearer if we notice another characteristic of the negative phase of the personal relation—its egocentricity. To be negatively motived is to be concerned for oneself in relation to the Other. The relation cannot be annulled; and the reference to the Other, since it is constitutive for the personal, cannot be evaded. We need the Other in order to be ourselves. But in any relation, the focus of attention and interest may become centred upon self rather than on the other; and since this is brought about through the refusal of the other to respond to my need—or what appears to me to be my need—my negative attitude defines the other as a danger to myself. This egocentric attitude has often been referred to as 'self-love', through failure to draw the distinction between positive and negative motivation. Self-love is self-contradictory. Love is necessarily for the Other, and self-love would mean self-alienation. But fear of the Other is fear for oneself, and involves a concentration of interest and activity upon the defence of the self. The role of the negative phase in the development of the personal relation is therefore the development of individuality. It is the phase of self-assertion, self-consciousness and self-development, in opposition to the Other. Its general ideal, which necessarily contains an element of illusion, is independence of the Other and self-sufficiency.

The child, at any of the critical stages of his early development, when forced into the negative phase by the mother's refusal to do for him any longer what he has come to expect, will, *in fact*, learn to do it for himself. He will, *as a matter of fact*, grow up and come to play the part required of him, stage by stage, until he reaches the independence of maturity. But this does not mean that he has developed satisfactorily, and even the skill and capacity which he shows in his adult occupations, whether of body or mind, is an inadequate measure of the success of his education. For these are functional—and therefore negative—aspects of his personal life, and the defining, positive aspect is his relation to the Other, and at the centre of this his relation to other persons. His quality as a person is the quality of his personal relations; and since a person is an agent, this means the character of the persistent system of motives which determines his personal relations. The formal aspect of this is the question whether his activities are in general negatively or positively motived, and it is this question upon which we must concentrate our attention.

The mother's refusal of what he expects from her confronts the child with a contradiction in his consciousness, which has various aspects. The primary aspect is practical, as a clash of wills. Hitherto, his expectation has been regularly fulfilled. He has learned to expect, that is, to imagine in advance, to refer a present symbol to a future occurrence. Now he goes on imagining a future which does not occur and the longer it is postponed the greater becomes his fear and the more vivid his expectation. The expectation, persistently unfulfilled, becomes a demand. His cry for what he expects passes into an angry insistence, even perhaps into a paroxysm of rage. This is the genesis of will, which always implies a self-assertion against the Other, an opposition to be overcome, and therefore an awareness of self as opposed to the Other. This conflict of wills individualizes the child for himself; and the mother who opposes him, for him. He recognizes himself as an agent through the opposition of another agent, who seeks to determine his future against his own will.

This exposition should not be taken as determining a particular point in a child's development at which self-consciousness supervenes upon a consciousness of an earlier kind. It is to be taken generally and diagrammatically. The distinction of Self and Other is present from the beginning, since the infant, being dependent totally upon the mother, must wait upon the other person for the satisfaction of his needs. There is a necessary time lag between the consciousness of need and its satisfaction. But so long as the expectation is not disappointed, so long as there is a regularity in the recurrence of the supply of his needs, there is no crisis which concentrates attention upon himself by compelling him to make a demand instead of merely waiting passively. At most there is a point in personal development, which may vary considerably from child to child, at which the contrast between Self and Other is finally established as a pervasive attitude in action and reflection.

The negative aspect of this contradiction in consciousness establishes the reflective distinction between good and bad, and between true and false. The mother's refusal institutes a dichotomy in the child's consciousness between what he expects and what actually occurs; between his demand and the response to it. He is forced into a recognition of the distinction between imagining and perceiving. For what he anticipates in imagination is contradicted by what actually takes place, and this institutes the contrast between phantasy and reality. But here we must remember that this happens in action and that the Other is personal. Both sides of the distinction are referred to the Other. What is imagined is what is demanded of the Other. What occurs is something distinct from what is demanded, which the Other actually does. The contrast of what is imagined with what is perceived is an aspect of the conflict of wills. It is indeed the knowledge of this conflict. The distinction between what is imagined and what is perceived represents, in the consciousness of the individual, the contradiction between his own will and the will of the Other; between what he intends that the Other should do and what the Other intends and does. To recognize this distinction is to recognize one's own frustration.

Now what the child expects the mother to do is what, relatively to his knowledge, would satisfy his need. It is, then, what she ought to do, but will not. So his mother is wicked. In his fear for himself he is angry with her and hates her. Yet this hate and anger depend upon his need of her love, and his memory of the time when he and she loved one another. Moreover, the situation in which he finds himself, and the state of mind into which he is come, is one which is dreadful to him and from which he needs to escape. Yet he can only escape from it, it appears to him, if she will change her mind, and be good to him again. Then he will forgive her and they will be reconciled: they will be friends again and enjoy one another.

Within this contradiction of will and feeling the purely factual distinction between true and false is contained. For there is in it a conception of the order of the world, however simple and unaffirmed, and an expectation based upon that conception, which has proved false in the event. This distinction, however, is still implicit; it is derivative and subordinate. For the Other is personal, and the order of events on which memory bases expectation is the past actions of the mother in caring for her child. The personal relation is primarily practical. His mother has played him false by acting wrongly. We have seen that the distinction between right and wrong is inherent in the nature of action.[1] We see now that this distinction, without which there can be no action, but only reaction to stimulus, is involved in the original structure of human motivation; and that it has its ultimate moral reference through the personal relation which constitutes the human individual a person. What we are here considering is the origin of the moral struggle, in a situation which is universal and necessary in human experience. This

[1] *The Self as Agent*, p. 140.

situation is the conflict of wills between mother and child. The moral struggle is primarily a struggle between persons. It is only secondarily, though also necessarily, a struggle within the individual. For the motivation of the individual and the consciousness which it contains, has reference to the Other. He needs the Other in order to be himself; and his awareness is an awareness of the Other. Consequently, if his relation to the Other becomes negative, the conflict is reflected in himself. He must maintain the relation even in rejecting it: he cannot escape from it except by escaping from himself. His relation to the Other becomes ambivalent. He is divided in himself, fearing and therefore hating what he loves, turned against himself because he is against the Other. From this conflict of agents are derived all the characteristic dichotomies in terms of which human life must be lived, and in it they are contained. With their emergence in consciousness, as distinctions between real and unreal, right and wrong, good and evil, true and false, action becomes necessary and human life becomes problematic. We are compelled to distinguish and to choose.

These reflections upon the formal structure of the moment of withdrawal in personal development do not merely disclose the origin of the ultimate distinctions which make human life problematic. They reveal the form of the basic problem itself. In its largest scope it is the problem of reconciliation. From the standpoint of the individual it is the problem of overcoming fear. Think again of the child's situation. He is refused what experience has given him the right to expect, and his cosmos has returned to chaos. He is obliged to do something for himself which his mother has always done for him. His mother compels him to do it. But we must notice that this compulsion is not a physical compulsion. It is in the nature of things impossible to compel another person to act, if by compulsion we mean a merely physical necessitation. The capacity to act is freedom. The most we can do is to provide another with a sufficient motive for doing what we want him to do. The motive, however, may be negative. We may make him afraid not to do what we demand of him. The child is in this case. His need for his mother is absolute; his fear for himself refers to this need for the mother's care. Consequently, he has a sufficient motive for doing what she requires, however much against his will.

Now if this is what happens; if the child learns to do what is required of him for fear of the consequences to himself, he has failed to make the return to a positive motivation from the negative phase of withdrawal. The negative motive remains dominant. He is still on the defensive. He has indeed returned to the field of action; but he acts from negative, and, therefore, egocentric motives. He has learned to do something for himself, but for his own sake; and his individual character is by that much more negative.

If the return from the negative phase is to be completely successful it is necessary that the dominance of the negative motive be completely overcome, and that the positive relation to the mother be fully re-established, in spite of her continuing refusal to satisfy his demand. It is the conditions and implications of such a successful overcoming of fear that concern our study. We may sum them up by saying that they consist in recognizing the illusions involved in the negative phase, and as a consequence the disappearance of the conflict of wills. This recognition of illusion does not necessarily involve its expression in judgment, and in the earliest stage of our development it cannot do so. To recognize as unreal what has been taken as real is to reverse a valuation, and value, we have seen,[1] is primarily felt. The 'facts' of the situation remain unchanged. What is required for the recognition of unreality is a change of feeling from negative to positive (or vice versa), coupled with a memory of the earlier attitude.

The judgment which would express the child's attitude in the negative phase is this. 'Mother doesn't love me any more'; or, as it hardens into definiteness and arouses the will, 'Mother is against me.' It is this feeling that constitutes the negative relation of persons, and it is therefore mutual. 'If Mother is

---

[1] *The Self as Agent*, p. 190.

against me then I am against her.' Now to overcome this negation, it is necessary that the judgment should be reversed, and its reversal involves the recognition that it was illusory. The further judgment must be 'Mother appeared to be against me, but she wasn't really.' This primary recognition of the distinction between appearance and reality carries certain fundamental implications, however long it may take a child to recognize them fully. Of these, we may notice two which are of fundamental formal significance. The first is the implication that he was wrong; that his feeling, and so his valuation, of the Other, was mistaken. We might formulate this by saying, 'I thought Mother was bad, but she wasn't. She was good. It was I who was bad.' This provides the formal basis of moral experience. The second implication provides the formal basis of intellectual experience—the distinction between true and false. The child recognizes in action, if not yet in reflection, that his expectation was based upon too limited an experience. His conception of the 'uniformity of Nature'—as we are used to calling the repetition of the same—was too simple. What appeared to be constants have turned out to be variables. Thus the disappointment of expectation based upon the experience of an invariant sequence in the behaviour of the Other provides the experience of being in error. But with regard to this implication, we must note that it is relatively independent of the pattern of motivation and the rhythm of its changes. Whether the child succeeds or fails in overcoming the negation in his relation to the mother he must recognize that his expectation has been falsified. Here he is dealing with mere matter of fact. For this reason our knowledge of the impersonal aspect of our world is always relatively independent of our feelings, attitudes and motives. I say 'relatively' because the activities through which we gain such knowledge can never be independent of the motives which sustain them. These motives, though they may have little relevance to the truth or falsity of the conclusions we reach, still determine the direction of our attention; and so the kind of questions we ask, to which our conclusions are the answers.

The return from the negative is not, then, necessarily achieved in its completeness, or satisfactorily. If it were, the original positive relation of mother and child would be re-established fully at a higher level; a level at which the child has learned to trust the mother in spite of appearances, and at which he has something to contribute of his own initiative to the common life. Instead of doing what he has learned to do for himself, from fear of the consequences, he would do it for the mother, in co-operation with her, and so as an expression of their mutual affection. The critical evidence of such a satisfactory return to full positive mutuality would be the complete disappearance in the child of any desire for the earlier stage which he has out-grown, of any hankering after more infantile expressions of affection. But such a success is beyond the bounds of all probability, at least as a continuing achievement in all the repetitions of the rhythm of withdrawal and return which make up the personal development to maturity. It may be achieved, or nearly achieved, upon occasion, but on the whole and on balance the most we can hope for is a qualified success. The main reason for this lies in the mother. A complete success would only be possible if the mother's relation to the child was and remained continuously fully positive and free from egocen-tricity. Her task in the development is to convince the child, without going back upon her refusal to give him what he demands, that his fear that she is against him is an illusion; and that she refuses what he wants wholly for his sake, and not at all for her own. Even with the best of mothers this can be so only in the main, and never absolutely and continuously. So far as she falls short of this perfection of love, so far the child's feeling that she is against him is not an illusion; and by so much she must fail to overcome his negative attitude and to reinstate a fully positive relation.

Finally, then, we must consider the formal result of this general failure to overcome completely the negative motivation which sustains the phase of withdrawal, and consequently the illusions and contradictions which are inseparable from it. The failure must mean that the relation with the Other at the higher level is established upon a mixed motive. It contains an element of fear which is not integrated within the positive motivation of the return to action, but suppressed. This suppression is possible through a concentration of attention. The intention of an action, as we saw,[1] is bound up with the attention which selects the field of our awareness in acting. But no action can have contradictory intentions. We cannot aim in different directions at the same time. It can, however, have contradictory motives, one of which is suppressed, and therefore 'unconscious'. And since our actions contain a negative element which is in the same sense 'unconscious', the unconscious motive may find expression in action, so that we find that what we have done is not what we intended, but something different; even something opposite and contradictory to our intention. In our relations with other persons this ambiguity of motivation is felt as a tension and a constraint between us, and therefore in each of us.

For simplicity's sake let us return to the child, and consider only the extreme possibilities. In the phase of withdrawal he is obsessed by an unfulfilled expectation, which persists as a demand for its fulfilment. But he is faced with a demand from his mother which is incompatible with his own demand. His need for the mother is such that he needs must accede to her demand, and so accept, in practice, the new phase of active co-operation with her. In this return to co-operation, if the negative motive which sustains his own demand is fully overcome, the demand itself will disappear, the desire which sustains it will cease to operate, and he will find a full satisfaction in the new mode of relationship. The conflict between imagination and actuality—between his image of what should occur, and what actually does occur—is fully resolved. If, on the contrary, he accedes to his mother's demand because he must, and against his will, the tension of contradiction is not resolved. He remains egocentric and on the defensive; he conforms in behaviour to what is expected of him, but, as it were, as a matter of policy. In that case, he

---

[1] *The Self as Agent*, pp. 171 f.

cannot find satisfaction in the new forms of co-operation, and they remain for him unreal. His heart is not in them. Consequently, the desire, and the activity of imagination which it sustains, do not disappear. The contradiction between the imagined satisfaction and the unsatisfactory actual persists. If this condition becomes habitual by repetition—and it must tend to do so, because the earlier experiences of withdrawal and return tend to become models for those that follow—it will institute a permanent dualism between the ideal and the actual, which will be accepted by the negatively motived individual as normal. Here, then, is an account of the genesis of dualism as a habit of mind.

The child who has been forced back into co-operative activity without a resolution of the conflict has two courses open to him. He remains egocentric, and the objective of his behaviour is security, through self-defence. What he cannot do, so long as his fear is not overcome and dissipated, is to give himself freely to his mother in the fellowship of mutual affection without constraint. The conflict remains. He can either run away or fight. If he takes the first course, he will conform obediently and even eagerly to the pattern of behaviour expected of him. He will become a 'good' boy, and by his 'goodness' he will seek to placate the mother whose enmity he fears. In compensation for this submission he will create for himself a secret life of phantasy where his own wishes are granted. And this life of the imagination in an imaginary world will be for him his *real* life in the *real* world—the world of ideas. His life in the actual world will remain unreal—a necessity which he will make as habitual and automatic as possible. What importance it has for him will derive from its necessity as a support for and a means to his real life, which is the life of thought, the spiritual life, the life of the mind.

He may, however, take the other course. He may seek to impose his own will upon his mother. He may become a 'bad' boy, rebellious and aggressive, seeking to gain by force or cunning what is not freely given to him. In that case he will carry the conflict of wills into the world of actuality, and seek power over the Other. He will use his imagination to discover and exploit the weaknesses of those on whom he is dependent, and to devise techniques for getting his own way. The frustration of his aggressiveness and the penalties of his disobedience will then increase his hostility, and with it his efforts to find the power and the means to assert his own will successfully and to compel compliance with his demands. *His* real life is the practical life, the life of action as the use of power to secure his own ends by his own efforts. The life of the imagination is unreal in itself, and has value for him only as a means to success in the practical life.

When this failure to overcome the negative motivation is established, one or other of these two courses will tend to become habitual by repetition. Through this process—which is the critical centre of all education—there will be produced an individual who is either characteristically submissive or characteristically aggressive in his active relation with the Other. This contrast of types of disposition corresponds to the distinction drawn by psychologists between the 'introvert' and the 'extravert'. But because we are drawing the distinction for philosophical purposes, we must do more than accept an empirical classification. In particular, we must understand their relation to one another as aspects of the form of the personal. I must draw attention, therefore, in summary fashion, to a few major implications of the analysis.

These two modes of behaviour are ambivalent. They have the same motive and the same ultimate objective—fear for oneself in relation to the Other, and the defence of oneself against the threat from the Other. They are, therefore, ambivalent forms of negative or egocentric behaviour. No individual can conform fully to either type; and the same individual will on occasion exchange the one mode of defence for the other. The two type forms are, therefore, better regarded as extreme limits between which fall the actual dispositions of human beings; each one varying its place from time to time within these limits while having a place on the scale which is, on the whole, its characteristic position.

Secondly, both types of attitude—submissive and aggressive—are negative, and therefore involve unreality. They carry over the illusion of the negative phase of withdrawal into the return to active relationship. They motivate a behaviour in relationship which is contradictory, and, therefore, self-defeating. For the inherent objective—the reality of the relationship—is the full mutuality of fellowship in a common life, in which alone the individual can realize himself as a person. But both the dispositions are egocentric, and motivate action which is for the sake of oneself, and not for the sake of the Other; which is, therefore, self-interested. Such action is implicitly a refusal of mutuality, and an effort to constrain the Other to do what we want. By conforming submissively to his wishes we put him under an obligation to care for us. By aggressive behaviour we seek to make him afraid not to care for us. In both cases, we are cheating; and in both cases the Other is compelled to defend himself against our deception, even though it is a self-deception. Self-interested relation excludes the mutuality it seeks to extort. If it succeeds in its intention, it produces the appearance of mutuality, not the reality. It can produce, at most, a reciprocity of co-operation which simulates, even while it excludes, the personal unity which it seeks to achieve.

Finally, these two negative dispositions, however persistent they may be, are never unalterable. For they are not innate characters, but habits which have been learned. In principle, what has been learned can be unlearned; and empirical experience offers us many examples of the transformation of character, sometimes by a gradual change, sometimes by a sudden and dramatic conversion. The rhythm of withdrawal and return does not cease with the achievement of organic maturity; it is the permanent form of the life of personal relationship. The transition from the withdrawal to the return repeats itself indefinitely, and each time it is made there is a possibility that it should be made successfully.

CHAPTER FIVE

Morality and its Modes

So far we have sought to determine the structure of the personal by reference to the relation of a child to his mother in the process of his development to maturity. One of the main reasons for adopting this procedure is that it greatly simplifies the situation we have to analyse without forcing us too far away from the concreteness of empirical experience. The personal life of the child is very simple in comparison with that of the adult; and this makes it easier to apprehend the universal form which distinguishes the personal from the organic. The particular advantage we gained lay in the uniqueness of the mother-child relation in the early years of life, when the mother is the Other than oneself—the undifferentiated world to which we belong. With the discrimination of the Other, which begins very early, a complexity of personal relations obscures the simplicity of the relation to the Other. Already in the last chapter this identification of the correlate of the 'I' with the mother was beginning to wear an air of unreality and even to hamper our exposition of the development of the original form of motivation. For discrimination within the individual is, as we have seen, necessarily correlated with the discrimination of the Other. We ought, therefore, at this point, to comment summarily upon the form of the relation of the individual person to the discriminated Other.

It might be thought that there is no justification for identifying the original form of the personal relation, as we find it in the relation of mother and child, with the universal relation of every individual person to the world at all stages of his life. The familiar argument might be brought against us that a genetic account cannot guarantee the validity of its conclusion. But this would be a mistake. The form which we have been defining is the form which distinguishes the personal from the non-personal. Provided we have determined it correctly, the stage of personal development which we use for its discovery can make no difference. If this form were to alter in the process of personal development it would not mean that he had become a different kind of person, but that he had ceased to be a person and become something else. The question to which we have sought an answer is this: 'What makes any individual entity a person?' and such a question must have the same answer at any stage of his existence. We must not forget that our centre of reference is the Self as agent, and that time is the form of action. Nothing can exist at an instant, least of all a person. To exist is to endure for a time; and the person, being an agent, generates time as the form of his own existence. To ask the question, 'Am I the same person now that I was as a child?' is therefore nonsensical. It only seems to have meaning through a confusion of form and content. I am in almost every respect different from what I was as a child, but the truth of this remark presupposes that I am the same person as the child that I was. If I were not, it would then be untrue to say that I had changed in the process of development. What makes us prone to this kind of nonsense is the traditional view, which we have found reason to reject, that personality is a distinguishing characteristic which is acquired in the process of development.

The genetic account, which we have offered, therefore differs in no way from an analytic account of mature experience, so far as its formal conclusion is concerned. We have simply looked for the form of the personal in the earliest stage of personal existence because it is then at its simplest and least complicated, and therefore most easy to discern, and we have followed the earliest stages of its development because it is essentially a form of action, and so takes time to exhibit itself. It is no doubt true that a genetic account of the development of a belief provides no proof of its validity; though it is going much too far if we aver that it can throw no light upon the question of its validity. But we have been concerned not with the validity of beliefs, or indeed with particular beliefs at all, but with the genesis, as a necessary consequence of the original form of personal existence, of the formal distinction between real and unreal, of which the distinction between true and false is one aspect. We have discovered why the form of the personal necessarily makes human existence problematical, so that the personal life necessitates the effort to distinguish between the true and the false, the good and the bad, the real and the unreal; and to act *in terms of* these distinctions.

To this we may add a more empirical justification. The process of personal development is the formation of habitual modes of behaviour. All habits are learned; and they become habitual by a shift of attention which passes beyond them to the formation of more complex habits which they support and in which they are integrated. The system of personal habit has, therefore, a hierarchical structure, and the more highly developed habits rest upon and presuppose those which were learned earlier. For this reason, the original form of personal motivation prescribes the ground pattern of all personal behaviour. Though in principle all habits can be modified, the pattern of motivation which underlies the process of habit-formation itself must remain unalterable. From this there follows a corollary of the utmost importance. Since the original form of the personal—as a universal form of motivation—makes personal existence problematic, as a life of action in terms of a distinction between reality and unreality, it defines the form of the real, though not its content. It defines, that is to say, the implicit objective of all personal action as the achievement and maintenance of a fully positive relation to the Other; in other words, of a personal reality in relation, through the subordination of the negative to the positive.

The Other, in personal maturity, is a discriminated Other.

Very early in personal experience the relation of the child to the mother becomes his relation to the family and its possessions. This is not a replacement of the mother by the family, but a discrimination of the Other. The mother remains the personal unity of the family, in which other persons and things are distinguished by their relation to her. The child is related to brothers and sisters through his mother, and equally to his father through his mother. Later this unity of the family takes its place as one element in a more fully discriminated Other—the unity of the society to which the family belongs, and to which the family is related through the father. This ambiguity of the relation of father and mother is important for the psychologist and the sociologist, but need not occupy our attention here. We may notice in passing, however, that when the world —that is to say, the discriminated Other as a unity—is conceived personally, the conception is most naturally and most effectively expressed in terms borrowed from the family unity. The family, indeed, is the natural model for any more inclusive group of persons conceived as a personal whole.

With the discrimination of the Other a way of release lies open from that dualism of motives which arises through the failure to overcome the negative phase in the process of growing up. The tension between affection and hostility may find release by distribution. The positive motive may find expression in relation to one member of the group and the negative in relation to another. In the family, for example, the hostility of the child to the mother may be diverted against the father. Or two brothers may unite in hostility to another. Again, the whole family may be united by projecting their mutual hostility against an outsider; or the unity of a nation may be intensified by combination against an 'enemy' nation. The principle is too well known to require further illustration. But it is important to recognize its source and its universality. Because of the correlation of Self and Other, and the reference to the Other which is the original characteristic of personal motivation, a contradiction in oneself must imply a contradiction in the Other. The contradiction of motives in myself must divide the person's world into friends and enemies. So long as there is an unsubordinated residue of negative disposition in any person, he needs something in the Other against which it may operate. Yet since the unresolved hostility is an element of unreality in himself, it introduces an illusory element into his friendships and his enmities alike. For a common hostility makes the bond of friendship appear to be closer than it is; and the enmity is not aroused by its object but projected upon it, and has its origin elsewhere.

We have distinguished, then, three types of disposition which arise through the interplay of positive and negative phases in the process of personal development, and which tend through habitual repetition to become characteristic of the individual. One of these is positive; the other two are negative, and as ambivalent are dialectically opposite. Our present purpose is to consider their bearing upon the morality of action, and the modes of morality to which they give rise. From this point of view we shall refer to these three basic dispositions of the agent as 'categories of apperception'. The reasons for selecting this language require to be stated, and the consideration of these reasons will carry our investigation a stage farther.

Until now we have kept our attention fixed upon the motives of action to the exclusion of its intentions. This limitation must now be abandoned, since in the absence of intention morality cannot arise, and indeed there can be no action, but only activity. Consequently, though every action must have a motive, it is not determined by its motive. It is determined, as this specific action, by the operation of intention. Now intention is the positive or practical aspect of attention;[1] and attention determines our knowledge of the situation in which we are acting, and which we are altering, or determining farther, by our action. We are speaking here of that primary knowledge which is to be recognized as a dimension of action; and of the situation as we apprehend it at the point of action, which is the present. This apprehension may contain an element of error.

---

[1] *The Self as Agent*, p. 171.

We may misapprehend the situation. But we need not consider this now. What is important for us is that it is always a limited apprehension, even if it is correct within its limits. For attention is selective; and the selection is relative to an interest in the agent. In any situation we notice what interests us, and attend to it; for only this is relevant to our intentions. The rest of what is there presented for our perception is overlooked. It is irrelevant to our interests. It is this process—for the most part automatic and unconscious—which is described by the term 'apperception'. Our established or habitual interests function as dispositions to select from what is presented to us at any moment and to organize it in consciousness in terms of its relevance to our intention.

Most of our settled interests are empirical. By this is meant that they are established by particular experience, and vary from one person to another. The bird-watcher on a country walk notices the birds and attends to their activities. His companion, the botanist, notices unusual plants which his friend overlooks. But there are certain interests which are universal and necessary because they belong to the structure of personal experience. Indeed, there must be such original interests, if the process of apperception is to arise at all. For all perception involves apperception, since it involves selection and interpretation. Now action is primary, and since to act is to choose,[1] there must be presupposed in the agent, as the basis of action as such, a system of motives whose differentiations refer to the Other, and so provide the possibility for a differential apperception of the same Other, and so for a choice between contrasted intentions. Now as the bare form of choice, this can only be represented by the distinction between a positive and a negative apperception of the Other. The agent must act *with* the Other, since there can be no action in the void. But the Other is at once a resistance and a support to the agent; and therefore can be apperceived either positively as a support or negatively as a resistance, and the agent can accordingly act either for or

[1] *The Self as Agent*, p. 139.

against the Other. His relation to the Other demands action; but leaves him the choice between a positive and a negative response to the demand.

Now these universal and necessary forms of apperception bear the same relation to the empirical forms as do the categories in the Kantian theory to empirical concepts. The categories are presuppositions of the possibility of all cognition; they are universal and necessary (or in Kantian terminology, 'a priori') concepts which determine the general form of all our experience. In reflective or theoretical activity they determine the form of the questions we ask, and to that extent the form of the answers we find: yet they do not determine the answers. Similarly, our three universal and necessary dispositions are presuppositions of the possibility of action as such; and as 'a priori' motives, determine the way in which we apperceive the Other in action, and to that extent, determine the 'form' of our action, as our practical response to the situation as we apprehend it. For this reason we may call this original system of apperception 'categorical' and its three determinations 'categories' of apperception.

The three categories of apperception give rise to three 'ways of life', each of which has its own moral structure, and reflectively, its own conception of morality. There are, therefore, three distinguishable modes of morality, each rooted in one of these three categories. It is convenient to assign descriptive titles to the three categories in terms of the way of life to which they give rise. The positive apperception may be called 'communal', the two negative types 'contemplative' and 'pragmatic' respectively. The contemplative apperception is the submissive form, the pragmatic the aggressive form of negative apperception. These terms will be justified in the sequel; but first we must consider morality in general, irrespective of its modal differentiations.

Since action is choice, the distinction between 'right' and 'wrong' is inherent in the nature of action.[1] This is a particular

---

[1] *The Self as Agent*, p. 140.

case of the problematic of personal experience, and since action is primary, the fundamental case, at least from the standpoint of the individual agent acting. To act is to be active in terms of a distinction between right and wrong, and what is done is done rightly or wrongly. This statement, however, is still abstract, because it treats the agent as an isolated individual. But the individual is constituted by his relation to the Other; and we must give concreteness to our account by recognizing this fact. To act is to realize intention, but it is also to enter into relation with the Other. We must therefore say that to act is to realize intention with the help of the Other. This does not apply merely to the personal Other. I open a packing-case with the help of a screwdriver, as well as lift it with the help of another man. In other words, to realize my intentions, I must make use of the Other.

Action, then, involves a relation to the Other. This relation, however, is a practical relation. It is not matter of fact, but matter of intention. At any moment I stand in specifiable relations to everything in the world. This is matter of fact. But when I act I enter into relation with something other than myself in virtue of my intention. This is true even of reflective activities. It makes the difference, for instance, between seeing and looking. To look at something is to see it with the intention of knowing it, and this transforms the seeing from matter of fact to matter of intention. Such an intentional relating of oneself to the Other depends upon knowledge of the Other; and the rightness or wrongness of the action, since it must be through the instrumentality of the Other, or 'with the help of the Other', depends, in part, upon the rightness or wrongness of one's apprehension of the Other. I say 'in part', because it depends also upon acquired skill in using the Other for my purpose. To act rightly, I must know, so far as is relevant to my intention, both what the properties or characters of the Other are, and also how to use the Other as a means to my end.

In consequence of this, there are two ways in which an action can be wrongly performed, either through a misapprehension of

the Other—by misunderstanding the situation, for instance—
or through lack of skill in operation. Either of these may result
in failure to realize the intention of the agent; but they need not
do so; though if the purpose is achieved it will be, as we say, 'by
accident'. In particular, I may achieve my purpose clumsily,
with unnecessary effort, or in an inappropriate fashion, and all
these are modalities of 'acting wrongly'. Acting rightly, therefore, we may say, is either a matter of efficiency or a matter of
style; and we may note that both criteria can be used in the
valuation of any action, and that which of the two standards
is the subordinate one will depend on whether the end or the
means is subordinate in the intentionality of the action. For
there are actions which are performed 'for their own sake', as we
say. They necessarily have a goal—an end which is aimed at—
but the end is incidental in intention and the action is done as an
exhibition of skill.

Now neither of these two modes of rightness is *moral*. The
rightness which is a matter of efficiency is a technological rightness. Stylistic rightness, on the other hand, is aesthetic. It is
manifested in the freedom, ease and grace with which the action
is performed. Moreover, it is judged from the standpoint of the
spectator; since the agent must concentrate his attention on the
end, and the style of his activity, resting upon skill already
acquired, is a matter of habit. The agent's judgment is in terms
of success or failure, so long as he is in action. The aesthetic
judgment of rightness expresses, therefore, a contemplative
attitude; the judgment which is concerned merely to assess
efficiency is technological, and manifests a pragmatic frame of
mind. We should commonly call it 'practical', but this is apt to
be misleading, since it suggests that it is the full and appropriate
judgment of action. It is practical only in contrast to the judgment of style and through its exclusion. It seems better, therefore, to call it pragmatic, and to mean by this that its standard is
exclusively the success or failure of the agent to achieve his
object by whatever means he adopts.

We may notice here the much discussed question of the relation of the 'right' and the 'good' in reference to actions. When we judge an action pragmatically we tend to use the terms 'right' and 'wrong'; when we judge it contemplatively we tend to call it 'good' or 'bad'. If, in order to achieve precision, we propose to make this the standard usage, we are apt to do so in terms of the pragmatic distinction between means and end, and to conclude that the right is the means to the good. But this is incorrect, since what we are judging is an action; and the end, considered without reference to the means taken to achieve it, is not an action at all, but a state of affairs. If we wish to pre-scribe a standard usage for these terms, it would be more correct to say that we should call an action 'right' when we are thinking of it, from the pragmatic point of view, as a means adopted to realize a particular end; while the term 'good' should more properly be applied to the action contemplated as a whole. Since action is purposive, this whole must be an organic whole; that is to say, its wholeness depends upon the functional inter-relation of the elementary activities which constitute it, upon the balanced and harmonious combination of its parts. This correlation of the contemplative attitude with an organic or functional representation of the unity of its object is characteris-tic. Similarly characteristic of the pragmatic attitude is a mechanical or 'casual' conception of its object as a whole.

But this prescription for the precise differentiation of the usage of 'right' and 'good', though conceptually defensible, is all but impossible to maintain in practice. For, in general, the more skilfully an action is performed, the more likely it is to achieve the end proposed. The two modes of rightness are not really separable, and any action provides grounds for both types of judgment. The distinction is grounded in the attitude of mind from which we judge; and whichever attitude we adopt, we cannot exclude, we can only subordinate the other. A style which necessarily hindered the success of the action could not be judged good, even from a purely aesthetic point of view.

In this analysis of the rightness of action, we have been dis-cussing action from the standpoint of an isolated agent. This is clear from the fact that we have taken the intention of the agent for granted, and raised no question of *its* rightness. For the same reason the rightness of which we have been speaking, in both its modes, is not *moral*. The most obviously immoral action can be efficiently and skilfully performed. This recalls the conclusion in an earlier lecture that whatever a solitary agent did would be right because he did it.[1] And this led to a further conclusion—that the condition of the possibility of action is that there should be a relation of agents in one field of action; for without this there would be no reason for choosing one possible action in preference to another. An action is defined by its intention, and its absolute rightness must lie, therefore, in the rightness of its intention. But if the intention can itself be either right or wrong, the ground for this cannot lie in the agent whose intention it is, but in the Other. Further, it cannot lie in the Other as the means used by the agent to accomplish his intention, but only in the Other as itself intentional, and therefore in the personal Other. The moral rightness of an action, therefore, has its ground in the relation of persons. The moral problematic of all action—the possibility that any action may be morally right or wrong— arises from the conflict of wills, and morality, in any mode, is the effort to resolve this conflict.

The moral rightness of an action, it might be widely agreed, rises from the fact that the actions of one person affect, either by way of help or hindrance, the actions of others. In virtue of this relation the intention of an action, and not merely certain aspects of the action may be right or wrong. This is sometimes expressed by saying that morality is essentially social. This, we may agree, is true, but it misses an essential element in the truth by considering the agents as isolated individuals and the relations of their individual actions as accidental or extrinsic. We have seen that the individuality of agents in relation is merely the negative aspect of an intrinsic relatedness. The 'I' and the 'You' are both constituted by the personal relation.[2] The inten-

---

[1] *The Self as Agent*, p. 143.
[2] *Supra*, Chap. IV, p. 91.

tion of one particular agent is therefore inherently related to the intention of the Other, and not merely accidentally. Consequently, the morality of an action is inherent in action itself, and does not supervene in cases where a particular action has consequences which impinge in a critical fashion on the lives of other people. Let us try to express this issue as formally as possible.

In an earlier lecture, when we were considering action from the standpoint of the isolated agent, we found that action is the determination of the future.[1] We must now consider how this affects the agent when he is one of a group of agents related in the same field of action.

We must here bear in mind some of the major implications of the point of view which we have adopted. The theoretical standpoint, with its dualism of Subject and Object, compels us to think the world an Object and the identity of the Self as a unity of consciousness or thought. When we then seek to give some account of action, we credit the Self with some curious power to effect changes in the world by acts of will. The effect of this is that we think of our experience as a continuity of awareness, which constitutes the continuing identity of the Self in time. Occasionally, this continuum of consciousness somehow gives rise to acts which have casual effects in the external world, if a conscious decision to do so has been reached. These acts are then thought as atomic, connected with one another only through the fact that they are all separate acts of one and the same Subject. But when we exchange this point of view for that of the Agent-Self, postulating the primacy of the practical, and so escaping from dualism, the position is different. The world is now thought as a unity of action, and the self-identity of the agent is a continuity of action. What happens occasionally is that the intentionality of our action may be reflected back upon itself, and so produce a reflective activity, while the practical activity continues automatically, as a result of established habits.

[1] *The Self as Agent*, p. 134.

If, now, we replace the abstract conception of the Agent, by the group or society of agents, this society must be conceived as a differentiation of the Agent, and not as a set of individual objects. They have their being, as agents, in the continuum of action which is the World. If the whole society of agents is contrasted with the world as their 'Other', this does not deny that the society is part of the world: and if an individual agent contrasts himself with the society as his Other, even asserts his total opposition to the society, he does not assert that he is not a member of this society.

Now if the world is a continuum of action, and there are in it a number of agents; and if action is the determination of the future, the condition for action is a unity of intentions, and the actions of the different agents must be unified in one action. For the future of the World cannot be determined in incompatible ways. If it could be, the world would become, as it were, a plurality of incompatible worlds. Whatever actions are done in the world, it must remain one world. If then, two agents, or two groups of agents have incompatible intentions, both intentions cannot be realized. In this situation, either one agent must yield to the other, of his own free will, or they must seek to prevent one another from acting. In the first case one of the agents loses his freedom, and cannot realize his nature as an agent; in the second, both lose their freedom until one has mastered the other and forced him to abandon his intention. For in a struggle of wills action is negative, as we have seen. The intention of each party is dictated by the other, and neither determines the common future. The struggle, of course, may have quite catastrophic effects upon the situation, but the consequences are not *intended* by the agents in the struggle. We should notice that this will be the result whether the agents whose intentions are incompatible are in direct or indirect relation with one another. The success of an operator on the New York Stock Exchange may ruin a number of people in Germany or China.

This interrelation of agents, which makes the freedom of all members of a society depend upon the intentions of each, is the ground of morality. It provides a reference beyond themselves for all possible intentions in virtue of which they can be either right or wrong, and this rightness or wrongness is neither technical nor aesthetic, but moral. Its corollary is that the freedom of any agent—that is to say, his capacity to realize his own being as an agent—is conditioned, inherently, by the action of all other agents. *My* freedom depends upon how *you* behave. This provides an absolute, though only an indeterminate or formal criterion of morality.

If we call the harmonious interrelation of agents their 'community', we may say that a morally right action is an action which intends community. Kant has already formulated this in one of the moral modes by saying,'Act always as a legislating member of a kingdom of ends.' Any act of any agent is an expression of his own freedom. But if the world is one action, any particular action determines the future, within its own limits, for all agents. Every individual agent is therefore responsible to all other agents for his actions. Freedom and responsibility are, then, aspects of one fact. The intention of any agent is, however, relative to his knowledge of the Other. His responsibility cannot extend beyond his knowledge. Consequently, whatever he does is morally right if the particular intention of his action is controlled by a general intention to maintain the community of agents, and wrong if it is not so controlled.

Such a general intention is a unifying intention. Not only is it the intention which maintains the personal unity of any group of agents; but it also unifies the actions of an individual agent in a single life. For it is the intention which remains the same for all his actions, and to which they all have reference. It is a universal and necessary intention for all agents, since the relation of persons is constitutive for their existence as persons. They can only be themselves and realize their freedom as agents through their relation to one another. The interrelation of agents is a necessary matter of fact. But it is also a necessary matter of intention. For it is not enough to constitute the agent a person that he should in fact be a member of a group of persons. He must know that he is a member of the group, and that in all his actions he is entering into intentional relation, directly or indirectly, with the others. This universal and necessary intention, which is the same for all agents, because it springs purely from their nature as agents, provides, therefore, a norm for the rightness or wrongness of all actions whatever. It is this that enables us to define morality by reference to maintaining community in action.

It is to be noted that the moral rightness or wrongness of an action resides in its intention. This has two important consequences. The first is that it is independent of success or failure. The man who attempts to kill his neighbour and fails is morally guilty of murder, though not legally. The second is the one which concerns us more immediately. The negative aspect of intention is attention. This is simply a specification of the general principle that knowledge is the negative aspect or 'dimension' of action. In a particular action, the effective knowledge in it is selected by attention, just as the direction of the acting is selected by intention. Now any general type of selection in attention which is characteristic of a particular agent will constitute his normal mode of apperception; and in his personal relation with other agents it will be his normal mode of moral apperception, and will decide how he envisages the community of agents of which he is a member. It is to this knowledge that the rightness or wrongness of his intention in action is relative, and his moral responsibility is limited by it. Even if his conception of morality is an inadequate one, his intentions in particular are morally right if they exemplify it, and morally wrong if they negate it. An agent's morality must be relative to his own conscience.

Further, if a particular mode of apperception is generally characteristic for any community of persons, it will determine the moral outlook which is normal in that community, and consequently its moral orthodoxy. For any member of the community this will define what is expected of him as a moral agent by the community. It will generally, though not necessarily, define what it is right for him to do. Not necessarily, because his own moral apperception—that is, his conscience—may not be identical with the normal one; but generally, otherwise the moral orthodoxy in question would not be normal. Even where the conscience of the individual is unorthodox, however, it must be related to the orthodox code. For morality refers to the structure of personal relations which unites the members in a community of agents, and personal relations are necessarily reciprocal. What is expected of me by the Other must always play an important part, though not always a decisive part, in determining the morality of my actions.

The question of morality is even more complex than is already apparent. For we must distinguish the moral orthodoxy of any community from its traditional moral code. The code of morality which is traditionally proposed in any community may differ widely from the system of norms which in practice guides the behaviour of the majority of its members when they are acting conscientiously, and which determines what is expected of any member as a responsible moral agent. The morality traditionally professed may be ideal and theoretical; while the normal orthodox morality is practical and effective.

This brings us to our main point. If there are three categories of apperception, there must be three typical modes of morality which correspond to them. For a category of apperception will determine the form in which the community of agents is conceived. It will determine the form of the demand upon me to which my moral action is the response. In calling these modes of morality typical, what is meant is that they are formal possibilities; what is not meant is that one or other of them must completely characterize any individual or any community. In actual life all three may be found operative, either in the individual or in the orthodoxy of a group. What we can say is that one of the three will tend to be dominant, in any particular individual agent and in any group of agents at any time. The moral orthodoxy of a group *as a whole* will tend to be in one or other of the three modes. The reason for this tendency is that if they are mixed they will give rise to moral conflict, which can only be avoided if one of them is taken as normal for the others. There is a natural pressure towards system in practice as well as in theory, and the avoidance of conflict in personal relations is one of the functions of any moral orthodoxy. But we have to remember that a larger community may contain smaller communities within it, and the code of morality which is normal for the small community may be in a different mode from that which is normal for the larger. In other words, a man's apperception of his relations to the other members of his family may differ modally from his apperception of his relations as a citizen to other members of his State.

There are then three typical modes of morality, one based upon a positive apperception and two upon negative apperceptions which are opposite and ambivalent. It will be convenient to use the same terms to designate these modes as we assigned to the categories which gave rise to them. We shall, therefore, refer to the positive mode as 'communal', and the negative modes as 'contemplative' and 'pragmatic' respectively. We shall have more to say in the next lecture about their differences and their relation to one another. But before I break off, I should like to identify them, without discussing the reasons for this identification, in the moral tradition of Europe.

The communal mode, resting as it does on a positive motivation, is characteristically heterocentric. By this is meant that the centre of reference for the agent, when he seeks to act rightly, is always the personal Other. To act rightly is then to act for the sake of the Other and not of oneself. The Other, in this mode, always remains fully personal; consequently its objective must be the maintaining of positive personal relations between all agents as the bond of community. It is characteristic for this mode, then, that in the face of the moral problem, which is the problem of hostility resting upon fear, it demands the transformation of motives by the overcoming of fear. 'Thou shalt love thy neighbour as thyself' is then a normal expression of com-

munal morality. Equally characteristic, in relation to negative |
motivation in the Other, is the formulation, 'Love your enemies'.
We identify this mode of morality, in the European tradition,
with the moral disposition which has its origin in Hebrew culture, and which entered Europe through the spread of Christianity from Palestine. We should perhaps avoid calling it
Christian morality, though this would be strictly correct, because what is usually identified as 'Christian' morality is mis-
conceived in one of the negative modes.

The two negative modes are, on the contrary, both egocentric.
This egocentricity creates a dualism, as we have seen. For the
relation to the Other constitutes both oneself and the other;
the intention to maintain, in general, the relations that unite the
members in a community is a necessary intention. But the habitual motivation negates this. So for the negative modes of
apperception the world divides into two worlds; an actual world
which does not answer to our demands, and refuses to satisfy us,
and another world, an ideal world which we can imagine, which
does. Whether this gives rise to a contemplative or to a pragmatic mode of morality depends upon which of the two worlds is
thought as the *real* world, which, that is to say, is taken as being
for the sake of the other. Similarly, the self becomes two selves,
for each of which one of these two worlds is 'the Other'. There
is a spiritual self with a spiritual life and a material self with a
bodily life. The positive apperception, through its heterocentricity, escapes this dualism.

For the contemplative mode, the *real* world is the spiritual
world, and the *real* life is the spiritual life. Just as the child can
take refuge from the apparent hostility of the mother by withdrawing into a life of phantasy, so the adult can solve the problem of living in a world which appears dangerous by withdrawing
into reflection, and adopting the attitude of a spectator. He
cannot, of course, escape from the necessity of practical activity,
and the necessity of the relation of agents which this entails. His
dependence upon the Other is matter of fact. But he can cease
consciously to *intend* the practical life. He can seek to realize

himself in the private, isolated world of his own thoughts and feelings and imaginings. To do this, he must *conform* in practice, and make the practical life a means to the inner life of the mind. This is possible provided that, and so far as, the practical life can be made automatic, a matter of routine and habit, which supports as a whole a deliberate and intentional life of reflection, contemplation and ideal construction. He will engage in deliberate practical activity only because he must, and only so far as he must.

If this category of apperception is normal for any human society, the necessary harmony of the relations of its members in the practical life must then be made automatic. This is possible if there is established a common form which is unchanging, within which the activity of each member is adjusted to that of the others automatically. The form will be of an organic type, a system of social habit, in which the activity of each member is functionally related to the activity of the others, so that the practical life of the society is a balanced and harmonious unity, a system of social habit. To maintain this each member must have his function in the common life; he must be trained from childhood to recognize the social pattern and his own function in it, and to develop the system of habits which makes conformity to it a second nature.

The contemplative mode of morality is then a morality of good form. Wrong action is bad form; doing something that is not 'seemly', not 'fitting'. Its standard is, in the broad sense, an aesthetic standard. It is not the sort of standard that can easily be formulated in general precepts. It has to be felt. It is a kind of beauty or grace in social relations, a matter of style, of balance, of tact and poise. It displays a knowledge of how to behave which rests on insight or intuition, and cannot be reduced to general rules. It depends upon a vision of the good which is the same for all who are united in personal activity by means of it. We should be inclined to regard it as concerned rather with manners than with morals, but that is because our normal mode of apperception relegates it to a subordinate role in the realization of a harmony of action in society. For it pre-supposes that the real life is not the life of action but of reflection. The classical exposition of this mode of morality is Plato's *Republic*, and it is the normal mode of morality for the Class-ical Greek moralists.

The other negative mode, which we have called 'pragmatic', is the antithesis and the complement of this. If the material life —the life of action—is taken as real, then the life of the spirit is subordinate and becomes a means to practice. In that case the conflict of wills is met by aggression, by the effort to overpower the resistance of other agents and compel them to submit. If I apperceive life in this way, my goal must be the appropriation of power; and the relation of agents becomes a competition for power. The problematic of action becomes the effort to achieve my own purpose in the face of resistance from the other. But because of the interdependence of agents, this must be limited by the necessity to maintain the unity of society, that is, the sys-tematic co-operation of agents. A mode of morality is required which fits this apperception.

Now from this point of view all problems of action become technological. For the ends of action are taken for granted. Each individual has his own intention which he is determined to realize. His problem concerns the means to realize it in the face of resistance; it is efficiency in action that determines right and wrong. Now the *technique* for maintaining a harmony of co-operation in a society is law, conceived as a means for keeping the peace. The pragmatic mode of morality will then be con-ceived as obedience to law—to a moral law which the individual imposes upon himself, and through which he secures the univer-sal intention to maintain the community of action. It will be a morality of self-control, of power over the self, limiting its own freedom for the sake of maintaining the community. It will be expressed in terms of will, obligation and duty, as a set of rules or principles, which are the same for all, and which limit for each the use of his own power to do what he pleases. This mode of morality is too familiar to us to need further identification. It has its origins, so far as Western Europe is concerned, in the Stoic philosophy and Roman law; and its most brilliant exponent in the modern world has been Immanuel Kant.

CHAPTER SIX

Community and Society

The discussion of morality which formed the theme of the last chapter provides a bridge from the individual to the social aspect of the personal. Hitherto, though we have stressed the relation of persons, even to the extent of making it the matrix of personal individuality, we have looked at it from the standpoint of one of the related individuals. Morality is still, in this sense, characteristic of the individual. It is the individual in whom the demand to act morally arises, so that it is experienced as a demand that he makes upon himself. Yet its reference is to him as a member of a society of agents, and its function could not be fulfilled—indeed it would not be a *moral* demand— if it were not universal, if each member of the society did not make the same demand upon himself. It is this essential character of morality which led Kant to say that the moral individual, in acting morally, is legislating for all members of the Kingdom of Ends; acting in a representative capacity; acting for humanity in his own person. We must now cross the bridge which morality provides and look at the relation of persons from the social standpoint.

We must stress first a truth which we have already emphasized from the point of view of the individual. Any human society is a unity of persons. This means that its unity as a society is not merely matter of fact, but matter of intention. It cannot, therefore, be understood, or even properly described in biological terms. It is not a natural phenomenon. It is not an organic unity, even if it has a negative organic aspect. Its persistence and development is not 'teleological', not an evolutionary process. An evolutionary development moves from an original homogeneity to an increasing heterogeneity—as in the evolution of species. The history of human society, on the contrary, moves from an original heterogeneity to an increasing homogeneity. Its continuity is a continuity of action, not of process. Any human society, however primitive, is maintained by the intention of its members to maintain it. Short of the extermination of its members, it can be destroyed only by destroying this intention. The history of the Poles or the Czechs, or, above all, of the Jews, should be sufficient evidence of this. To seek its basis in a supposititious herd-instinct is merely puerile. Human beings have no instincts, and a human society is not a herd. Any human society is a moral entity. Its basis is the universal and necessary intention to maintain the personal relation which makes the human individual a person, and his life a common life. It is an instantiation of the 'I and You' as the unit of the personal. It is constituted and maintained by loyalty and keeping faith.

It has become a commonplace of theory that human life is essentially social. But this general agreement is highly ambiguous, and means quite different things to different people. As an explicit theory it emerges, in European history, as the answer that Plato, and following him, Aristotle, found to the disruptive dualism of the Sophists. 'Should men live by nature or by custom?' they asked. Plato answered that the dichotomy is absurd. For men, to live by nature is to live by custom. Human nature is social and custom is the bond of society. The Greek doctrine is most familiar in the form given to it by Aristotle, πολιτικὸν ξωόν ἄνθρωπος, 'Man is a political (i.e. a social) animal.' The generic definition of man as an animal we must totally reject. What Aristotle may intend by the term πολιτικόν and whether it is consistent with the generic term ξωόν (living creature) or not, we need not enquire. But on one easy interpretation, it yields a modern version of the commonplace that 'Man is one of the herd-animals.' In that case, the statement that man is social means that men live in groups, like the ants or the bees, like wolves or buffaloes, and they behave as members of a group. In other words, the unity that constitutes a human community is the same, in principle, as that which constitutes the community of a beehive. The difference is one of complexity, not of type. This interpretation of the social character of human life we must reject out of hand. It is the social version of the attempt, which we have already denounced, to understand the personal on the analogy of the organic. This is a rather crude instance of a misinterpretation which takes subtler forms. The underlying error which vitiates all such forms is that they treat human society as mere matter of fact, which can be observed and described from the standpoint of a spectator.

But surely, it may be said, this is quite possible. Why should it not be? There is, of course, a sense in which it is possible, since it has been done. There is even a sense in which it is valuable and necessary to do it—provided that we know what we are doing, the limits within which our results can be valid, and the qualifications which require to be made. But if such theories are offered or accepted as true without qualification, if they are believed to be, in principle, adequate accounts of the social character of human life, they rest upon and propagate an illusion.

The reason for this is quite simple. If I am watching a hive of bees, noting the purposiveness of their behaviour and the division of labour that characterizes their activity, I may form a theory of the principles which are at work to maintain this communal activity. My theory may be true or false, adequate or inadequate, but in any case it makes no difference to the bees, or at most only an accidental difference, if they take me for a dangerous intruder. But if I form theories about human society in the same fashion this is not the case. For I am not just a spectator of human activity, but a participant. Indeed, this search for understanding which leads me to form my theories is itself a characteristic human activity which has no parallel among the animals. If I really believe my theory, that is, if I integrate it with my behaviour as part of my knowledge in action, it modifies my behaviour as a member of a human society. If I refuse to act in conformity with my theory, I behave as if it were not true, and so provide evidence that I do not really believe it. Again, if the majority of my own society accept it, my theory becomes the normal conception that this society has of itself, and consequently modifies the general character of its social behaviour. If most of my fellow-members, however, reject it and continue to behave as if it were not true, then I can only insist that they are in error, a prey to antiquated superstitions; that their behaviour is irrational and misguided. I can only work and pray for their enlightenment.

In either case my theory falsifies itself. For it is a description, in general terms, of how human beings do in fact behave in society. If they accept it, their way of behaving is altered, and the theory no longer describes it, but only the way they used to behave. If they reject it, they behave as if it were untrue. But then it *is* untrue, for it purports to be a theory of how, in fact, they do behave. If it be said that they may accept it in theory, without altering their practice, the position is still worse. For then they must say that this doctrine of mine, though true in theory, would not work in practice. But it is precisely a theory of practice, and if it would not work in practice it is *ipso facto* a false theory. We are here, you may notice, very close to the origins of the dualism of mind and matter. It lies in the dominance of the negative in us, in the fear of the Other, and the illusion that is inseparable from this negativity. For our fear of the Other generates the desire to escape from the demands of the Other upon us, by withdrawing from action into another life, the life of the mind, in which we can exist as thinkers, and realize our freedom in reflection. If this could be, then we should be pure minds, and spectators of a world of activity in which our actions would be determined for us by laws not of our making. In the realm of thought we should be free, but our bodily life would be determined by the laws of that world of necessity from which we have escaped. The world of action would become an *external* world, a world of phenomena; that is to say, a *show*—

a dramatic spectacle which unrolls itself upon the stage for us to watch, to follow and to enjoy.

This is not indeed possible, but we can make it appear possible. We can deceive ourselves and produce the illusion of a pure contemplation. We have only to suppress from consciousness the motive of our reflection by turning our attention away from it; and our fear of the Other, turned back upon itself, becomes an adequate motive for this suppression. Then we still speak and behave as though thought were motiveless; as if it were a self-moving activity, a ghostly kind of perpetual-motion machine. Reason will seem to provide its own driving force; it will *be* thought in its complete detachment from emotion or desire. We shall achieve thought in its purity—completely disinterested thought. We shall identify ourselves with Pure Reason which moves by its own logical nature to the apprehension of the Truth, without possibility of error. And if our thinking leads us into palpable error, we can always lay the blame upon the body and its practical demands. We can tell ourselves that we have failed to detach ourselves sufficiently from the life of the body and from the prejudice that is inseparable from the effort to satisfy its desires.

All this is illusion and self-deception. Pure thought, if there could be such a magic, would be pure phantasy. A thinking which could not be false could not be true. For it would no longer be problematic; it would no longer be governed by any distinction between true and false, and its results could not be knowledge, for they could neither be believed nor disbelieved. Thinking is something we do. Thinking in terms of dualism is one way of doing it. Whatever we do and however we do it, we must have a motive. And we have uncovered the motive of dualist thinking. It is the desire to know the truth without having to live by the truth. It is the secret wish to escape from moral commitment, from responsibility. If all my actions are determined by the Other then the Other cannot hold me responsible. And since the Other, in the last resort, is personal, if I yield my will to the Other and let his will command my actions, then the intention of my actions is not mine but his, and his therefore the responsibility for seeing that it is right action.

It may be objected that in raising the question of motive I am abandoning philosophy for psychology, and falling into one of the fallacies which even a beginner should know how to avoid. To this I shall reply, first, that the motive of this objection is to defend the illusion by forbidding us to bring the question of motive to attention; second, that philosophy does not constitute itself, as a science does, by isolating a field of study, but by refusing all such exclusions and abstractions. A philosophy which excludes certain questions on the ground that they belong to the field of psychology is giving itself the form of science, and so becoming a pseudo-science. The questions it does raise will show themselves sooner or later to be 'nonsense questions', till in the end it finds itself with no content at all. What I am doing is to remove the limitation which results from adopting a purely theoretical standpoint and to reassert the inclusiveness of philosophy by thinking from the standpoint of action. If thinking is one of the things we do, then the question, 'What motive have we for doing it?' becomes an essential element in any philosophical account of thought.

We must return from this digression, however, to our question about the social nature of man. So far we have discussed only its objective or scientific interpretation, and this we have rejected in the form in which it claims to be complete and adéquate. We must now consider its philosophical interpretations; and for this purpose we need only refer to the conflict between realist and idealist doctrine in modern political philosophy. We shall find here that the distinction we have drawn between the three categories of apperception provides us both with a clue and with a basis of criticism.

It is curious and suggestive that the traditional philosophical analysis of society takes the form of a philosophy of the State. For the State is at best an aspect of society and many societies are in no sense political. Quite apart from special groupings for limited purposes such as literary societies, or societies for the advancement of learning, there are many instances of self-supporting and self-sufficient human societies which cannot, or can only with difficulty, be subsumed under the concept of the State. We might instance primitive tribes, the Hebrews of Old *Nuer.* Testament times, China before its modernization by revolution, and so on. The idea of the State is closely linked with the idea of power, and the symbolism of the State is predominantly military. We talk indeed of States as Powers—whether great Powers or smaller Powers. It seems doubtful whether what we call the city-states of ancient Greece were really States in our sense of the term. For us the State is a legal entity, whose limits are defined by the territorial boundaries of its legal authority. Yet even an idealist philosopher like Bosanquet, who is concerned to deny that society is based on force, and to maintain that its unity is a spiritual and not a material unity, entitles the work in which this thesis is so brilliantly sustained, 'The Philosophical Theory of the State'.

This modern tendency to identify society with the State, or at least to define society through the aspect of political organization, is strong evidence of a dominantly pragmatic apperception of the social bond. For we recognized the mode of morality which rests upon a pragmatic apperception by the central place it gives to the ideas of 'power' and 'law'. The historical explanation of this identification is not far to seek. We are the heirs of the Roman tradition; and the Romans, whose outlook was characteristically pragmatic, invented the State as we know it. They did this by conceiving law as a technology for keeping the peace, and by uniting in one society, by the administration of a homogeneous law, backed by force, peoples and tribes who were in most other respects, and especially in culture, heterogeneous. As a result, we tend to think that organization as a State is the criterion of a fully complete and mature society, and to treat societies which lack this character either as dependent groups within a State, or as immature and undeveloped societies which must, like minors, be educated into statehood under the tutelage of their adult neighbours.

COMMUNITY AND SOCIETY

Thomas Hobbes, the father of modern political theory, provides an almost perfect example of an analysis of society in the pragmatic mode of apperception. His account, though he has given it a genetic form, must be understood, as he himself admits, as a logical analysis of the nature of the State and not as a historical account of its origin. The analysis reveals that the persons who compose society are, by nature, isolated units, afraid of one another, and continuously on the defensive. This means that the motivation of each in relation to the others is wholly negative. Further, the mode of their negative relation is the aggressive mode. For each isolated individual uses all his powers to secure his own satisfaction and to preserve his own life; and in consequence the state of Nature is a war of every man against every man. Under these conditions a human life is impossible; what life is possible must be 'poor, nasty, solitary, brutish and short'.

But these aggressively egocentric individuals are rational beings, that is to say, persons. Consequently, they know that they can only be themselves, and live a rational life, if they are united in a society. As rational creatures—and Hobbes realizes this—they must intend to escape from the fear and hostility of the state of Nature. This is to recognize what we referred to in the last Chapter as the universal and necessary intention of all personal activity. But again, Hobbes's conception of reason is characteristically pragmatic. It is a technological reason, a capacity to adapt means to ends. So reason is the source of the laws of Nature, of which Hobbes provides a long list. Now as laws of Nature, these are *moral* laws, inherent in the rational nature of all men universally. And since reason is conceived pragmatically, they are the laws of a pragmatic morality. What Hobbes means is this: that since Man is rational, he recognizes the universal and necessary means for realizing his own interests, for living a rational life; and a rational life is one in which ends are long-term ends, to be secured only by foresight and planning ahead, in contrast with a mere animal life of impulse which must be lived from hand to mouth. Thus the effect of reason is to turn fact into right. Not merely does a man use all his powers to further his own interest, he is right in doing so, and under obligation to a moral law in so acting. But also reason shows him that it is his interest to sacrifice momentary satisfaction for a greater long-term satisfaction, and he is under an obligation to use his power *rationally*, and so to limit its expenditure in obedience to a technological principle. To act rationally is to use the right means to secure his ends, and the right means are those which will in fact secure them, and secure them with the least expenditure of energy. Now there is a general condition of this which is of universal application. Action involves co-operation with the Other, and it is *impossible* to live rationally unless this co-operation is forthcoming. There must be a general agreement to limit the general aggressiveness in accordance with an agreed plan, and we must all keep the agreement. Making and keeping agreements is therefore a law of nature and so a moral obligation on every rational being.

There is, however, a final step in the analysis. The law of nature, which is the law of reason, or the moral law, would be ineffective if the conditions of acting in accordance with it were absent. 'Ought', as Kant said, 'implies can.' 'The laws of Nature', said Hobbes, 'bind only *in foro interno*', that is, they bind every man to the wish to live in accordance with them. This amounts to the same thing as Kant's principle. It only seems to be different if we take it to refer to an actual state of affairs, and not to an imaginary situation produced by analytical abstraction. Hobbes does not mean, as has been sometimes said, that I am under no obligation to keep an agreement if I think it would pay me better to break it. He means that I cannot keep an agreement unless the other party does so too. For an agreement which one of the parties does not intend to keep is not an agreement at all, but a stratagem in the war of every man against his neighbour. If the inward law is to be an effective obligation, I must have a guarantee that all the others intend to obey it. Even if my fear of the Other is illusory, so long as it exists I cannot keep the law, but must defend myself. Now since all men are motived by fear of the others, the only guarantee I can have is to know that the others will be more afraid to break the agreement than to keep it; and this can only be so if there is a power, external to all of us, which can compel all of us to keep the law. This is the power of the sovereign State, and the existence of this power makes society possible. It does this by equating self-interest and rational obligation. It is a pragmatic device which ensures that it should be in the interest of each of us to act in accordance with the law of reason. This alone can provide the sense of security which suppresses the fear of the Other and removes the necessity for self-defence. The power of government defends each individual against the self-interest of his neighbour. Given this situation, the moral law of reason becomes automatically binding *in foro externo*; becomes an obligation to act in accordance with it. For the power of the sovereign provides the conditions which make this possible.

It has been necessary to restate the logic of Hobbes's analysis at some length because it has been consistently misrepresented by its idealist critics. The liberal democratic tradition finds it a revolting theory, immoral and cynical. This emotional prejudice blinds us to the truth that it contains. It comes far closer to the normal ideal of our social practice than we are prepared to admit. Though Hobbesism has been violently and triumphantly exposed and disproved by most modern social theorists, it seems to possess a vitality which refuses to succumb. The reason is that it dares to provide a rational defence of the practice of a competitive society which in theory we find it emotionally necessary to disown. For a dualism of theory and practice is characteristic of Western society, and necessary to maintain it. We must therefore defend ourselves against any theory which expresses, consciously and in a rational form, the immanent ideal of our social practice.

Instead, then, of criticizing Hobbes in the familiar way, we must seek to relate his account of the social nexus to our account of the nexus of personal relationship. We can do this by saying that so far as the normal mode of moral apperception in an actual society is pragmatic, so far as its members are negatively motived in their relations and aggressive or 'practical' in their behaviour, the necessary unity of society can only be achieved by law backed by force. Its members are negatively charged particles which mutually repel one another. To hold them together an 'impressed force' is required, strong enough to overcome their centrifugal tendencies. Hobbesism, therefore, is the logical formulation of one of the three possible type forms of human society—the pragmatic type. Actual societies will approximate to this type in proportion as the motivation of their members is negative in relation to one another, and their intentional activity is practical rather than reflective. Under such conditions the unity of society must be based upon enlightened self-interest.

The pragmatic mode of society, then, is society maintained by power, and it identifies society with the State, since the power of government is a necessary condition for the existence of such a society. It conceives the structure of society in terms of law—whether moral or civil law—and its maintenance as achieved by power. This yields a mechanical concept of society. Its components are atomic units, inherently isolated or unrelated, and ideally equal. The units are dynamic; they are units of energy. There is nothing in them to hold them together. They are united in a whole by an external force which counteracts the tendency of their individual energies to repel one another. But as rational individuals who need one another, they themselves establish the power which unites them. Even Hobbes founds the absolute power of Leviathan upon the Will of the People. Law, backed by force, is the technical solution of the problem of a society of persons, and the creation of the State is the highest achievement of technological reason, of our human capacity to devise efficient means to achieve our natural ends.

The form of society antithetical to this pragmatic mode can be best realized by considering the form of criticism which historically has been brought against it. This criticism admits the logical brilliance of Hobbes's argument, but denies the premise on which it is based. This premise is the Hobbesian conception of human nature. The criticism may be put most stringently by saying that Hobbes is wrong in thinking that there is nothing in human nature to act as a bond of unity between man and man. The historical form of the argument against Hobbesism is that benevolence is as natural to man as self-love. But we must interpret this contention in the light of our own conclusions about human motivation. We must therefore notice the dualism in Hobbes's conception—a dualism which we will expect to find associated with all negative apperception. It takes the form of a contrast between human nature and human reason. Human nature is the nature of man if we leave reason out of account—his 'animal' nature. This contains all the motives of human behaviour: reason, as the capacity to think, does not determine the ends of action, but only the means to these ends. This dualism is, in fact, the Stoic dualism between Reason and the Passions in one of its modern incarnations. The criticism of Hobbes is concerned then with his view of human motivation, with man's 'animal' nature, and not with his rational nature. We might restate the usual criticism in the following form. Hobbes takes too low a view of human motives and too high a view of human reason. Because his conception of human motives is completely negative and egocentric, he is compelled to throw on human reason a task which it is too weak to undertake. Unless the natural tendencies of human behaviour themselves provided a bond of society, reason itself could never construct the State. Consequently, one has only to show that man's animal nature provides already a bond of unity between man and man to refute Hobbesism.

Now even the behaviour of animals cannot be explained by reference to mere individual self-preservation. We note a tendency to behaviour which promotes the welfare of the species; and a mother bird may even sacrifice her life for her brood. The same tendency—quite apart from any reasoning—is even more obvious among human beings. It is quite natural for a man to go out of his way to help a stranger in difficulties, and even the report of the sufferings of people whom we do not know tends to distress us. People enjoy being together and working together, quite apart from any calculation of self-interest, and even at times against their private interests. The war of all against all is at best an abnormal state of affairs, and a man with no interests whatever in the fortunes of his fellows is a freak of nature, and hardly human.

These facts are not disputable, and instances can be multiplied at will. Their philosophical interpretation, however, is another matter. For, firstly, we have learned to distrust biological analogies. From the observed facts of animal behaviour nothing follows for personal relations. Secondly, the question is whether the motive for such 'benevolent' activities, whatever it may be, is sufficiently constant, permanent and general to serve as a normal support for a life of corporate activity. Could it bear the strain of situations in which self-interest has patently and persistently to be set aside? Thirdly, not even Hobbes denies that men need one another, and have an interest in maintaining society. On the contrary, he asserts that the need for society is so fundamental in all of us that we will go to almost any lengths to escape from the state of Nature, and suffer any injustice short of a threat to life itself rather than return to it. What Hobbes maintains is that society is grounded wholly in our rationality, and not at all in our animal impulses. Finally, the fear that underlies the war of every man against every man is not a particular fear arising from a particular apprehension of danger, but a pervasive anxiety. Living as we do in an established society, this fear remains unconscious, being counterbalanced by the effectiveness of the law of the State. It is a mistake to think that Hobbesism implies absolute monarchy, although in the circumstances of his time Hobbes used it so. It demands a government with sovereign authority, established by the will of the people, possessing power commensurate with its authority, which is likewise derived from the people. Hobbes's argument that to change the government would involve a relapse into the state of Nature, overlooks the part played by habit in human behaviour.

The habit of social life is enough to sustain society during a change of government, provided the process is itself a habit and does not take too long to accomplish. We might add that Hobbes's estimate of human nature is far closer to the Hebrew-Christian tradition than that of his optimistic liberal opponents. It might be a sermon on the text which reads, 'The heart of man is deceitful above all things and desperately wicked.'

The antithesis to Hobbes is Rousseau; and to the persistent Hobbesism which runs through modern society the antithesis is the liberal humanism which derives from Rousseau and the Romantic movement and which finds its theoretical expression in the idealist theory of the State. Formally, this anti-Hobbesism rests upon the same dualism between rationality and human nature, but inverts their relation. Human nature is inherently good; if its expressions are perverted, the reason lies in the artificiality of existing social structures, which prevent it from expressing itself freely. Now, in principle, what is artificial is the product of artifice—that is to say, of reason conceived practically as the capacity for constructing artifacts. Consequently, Rousseauism finds the bond of society in man's 'animal' nature and the source of hostility and conflict in reason. The way of salvation lies in getting back to 'Nature', and allowing the natural goodness of human impulses to determine the form of society. Reason, then, has a negative function—to hinder hindrances to the good life: to hold the ring for the free play of natural impulses, 'taking men as they are', as Rousseau says, 'and States as they ought to be'.

The paradox that this involves runs through all idealist theory and shows itself most evidently in a continuous effort, which cannot be successful, to identify what *is* with what *ought to be*. The mechanism of this effort is a dialectical logic. Society is organic. If it is not *actually* so, it *ought* to be; and this means that it necessarily will be. For being organic it grows, and its present tensions and conflicts only *appear* to contradict this. They are its growing pains: the conflict of opposites is, indeed, the force which keeps society on the move, and compels it to develop towards its full organic maturity. Progress is then inevitable; it is a natural process, and the conservative effort to stabilize the *status quo* is only the negative phase of the tension by which society progresses. The evils we deplore are both necessary and yet unreal. They are necessary as phases in a development. They are unreal because they are transitory. The full manifestation of the reality of human society lies at the end of the process of development. This is not yet actual, but it is the ideal. We can know it in idea; and the ideal is the real.

Now since we are society at its present stage of development, and since reason can reveal the meaning of the process and enable us to grasp the reality to which the whole process inevitably moves, what we really want, as members of society, is the realization of this end. Our frantic efforts to resist the actual, and to escape from its tensions and conflicts, arise from the desire to have the future harmony here and now. So we confuse the present appearance with the reality to be manifested. We are like children who want to be grown up before their time, and who demand the right to behave here and now as if they were already adults. If we will only identify ourselves with the ideal end, which is the reality to which the progress of society tends; if we identify our individual wills with the general will of society, then we will find our present satisfaction in performing our own function in the social whole, and seek to do our duty in our own station. We will be able, in Rousseau's vivid phrase, to 'live in one generation and enjoy in the next'. We will act from our general will as members of society, willing the general good, not from our particular wills as individuals seeking vainly to secure their immediate individual interests. And since our being is really a social being, and our existence as independent individuals is an illusion, the general will is our real will, and our will for private self-interest is only a distorted appearance.

Now it is transparently clear that this conception of society is based on a contemplative apperception, just as the Hobbesian is based on a pragmatic apperception. Here is the child in the negative phase of the relation with the mother who submits to the mother's will, does what is expected of him, and compensates for giving up his own self-will in a world of phantasy. The idealist conception of society is rational, of course, while the child's phantasy world is mere imagination. But the mode of apperception is the same. In the dualism between the world of action and the world of idea, it is the ideal world that is the real, and the actual world that is appearance. Its rationality lies in the reference of the ideal to the actual; and this reference is achieved by taking the ideal world as the anticipation of the end to which the actual world automatically tends. So the world of practice is the means to the world of ideals. The only rational behaviour in practice is to submit to the Other, because whether I submit or resist makes no difference in the end. The Other is stronger than I, and will achieve its purpose in either case. It is therefore irrational to resist, both in the theoretical and in the practical sense. It is both stupid and wicked. For if I struggle against the Other, I shall only make a lot of unpleasantness for myself and for other people, and I shall gain nothing by it.

The self that apperceives life in this fashion is an isolated and therefore a divided self. He is at once a spectator-self and a participant-self. But his real life—his own private life—is as a spectator. Social history is a drama which unrolls itself before him, and which he watches and understands. But he also has a part to play upon the stage. In his public capacity a role is assigned to him, and it is his task to play his role properly; and he can only do this by suppressing his own self-expression and acting in the way that the author of the drama intended the part to be played. He must identify himself with his role—his station and its duties—and suppress his impulse to be himself. He can be himself only as a spectator, not as an actor.

In the contemplative mode of apperception, as in the pragmatic mode, the conception of society remains fundamentally negative. Its members are isolated individuals, whose real life is private and separate; yet for each of them the protection of society is necessary. How can they be united in a life of association without each losing his identity? Rousseau's formulation of

142

the problem cannot be bettered. 'The problem is', he says, 'to find a form of association which will defend . . . the person and goods of all the associates, and in which each, while uniting himself with all, will remain as free as before, and obey only himself.'[1] The answer to this problem, in all its many disguises, remains essentially the same. It is possible to have such a society by a mystical self-identification with the whole of which I form part. This is the clue to the mystery of self-government. I use the term 'mystical' advisedly, and not in any derogatory sense. Mysticism is an essential element in all reflective experience, though it is not usually recognized as such, because its role is normally subordinate. It is, however, essentially contemplative, and, in form at least, aesthetic. Self-identification with the whole, with the Other that includes oneself, is mysticism. The dramatist identifies himself with characters in his drama; so do the actors on the stage as they play their parts in the drama, and the spectators as they watch the spectacle, each remaining himself the while. But this is only theoretically possible—only in a play. If it is made the basis of society and so of life as a whole, it creates illusion. For then there is no other life than the life of the stage. We cannot leave the theatre and resume the serious business of *real* life where we must bear our own identities. The drama, whether comedy or tragedy, may be meaningful. It may comment upon life with the insight of genius. But if life itself is only a performance, tragic or comic as we please to take it, there is nothing for it to illumine. It can hardly be—for the members of the troupe, at least—a commentary upon itself. It becomes inherently meaningless and pointless.

Unlike the pragmatic society, the contemplative society is not a State. It is not grounded in power, but in the voluntary submission of its members to the general will. Its inherent ideal is anarchism—an automatic harmony of wills produced by the suppression of self-interest in favour of the moral will for the general good. In its modern form it is the Greek society plus the idea of progress, as a law of nature. Both Aristotle and Rousseau

[1] Rousseau, *The Social Contract*, Book 1, Chap VI.

recognize its limitation. It must be small enough for all its members to know one another and to meet together to take corporate decisions which express the general will. Otherwise the mystical identification becomes too tenuous to sustain the stresses of practical life. In a larger association, the device of representative government may appear to enlarge the scope of such a society, by an extension of the mystique of self-identification. The people choose representatives who do for it what it would do for itself if it were small enough. The chosen representative will identify himself with the constituency he represents, and speak with its voice. The fiction of self-government is thus still maintained. What emerges from the conflict of debate is the Will of the People, and that each of us, in obeying the law, remains free, and governs himself. The struggle of parties is not a struggle for power—it only appears to be. It is only a struggle of opinions; for all parties are equally seeking the common good, and the conflict of opinions is the dialectical method by which what is, here and now, the common good is brought to light. And when it is so revealed, it is loyally accepted by all as the will of the people, with which they identify themselves.

Government, or the State, is still necessary, but it is not society but merely a function of society, serving the general will for certain limited and defined purposes. It is needed for external defence; to judge between competing claims in accordance with the law that expresses the common will for the common good; and to administer the common services in the co-operative life. There is, of course, tension. There is struggle, of course, in every aspect of life. But the struggle is not *real*. There is no hostility in it. It has the character of a game. And it retains this character so long as all the players play the game and don't really play to win; so long as they are equally satisfied whether they win or lose. Of course, if any member of the society refuses to identify himself with the whole, and plays for his own hand, he must be taught the rules of good form, and if necessary forced to toe the line. But even this is only *apparently* a violation of his freedom. In reality he is being 'forced to be free'.

But here is the rub. This kind of society depends on the great majority of the members not taking the practical life seriously, but treating it as a means merely to the private life, the life of the spirit. And, in fact, whatever view they take, action is primary. To act as if this were not so is to live in an illusion. And the illusion is only possible by keeping theory and practice apart. It involves a belief that what is true in theory would not work in practice. The identification is itself merely ideal: and it can produce only the appearance of unity, not the reality. The practice of such a society may be worse or better than its theory, but it cannot be the expression of it. For the theory is really a compensation for the unsatisfactory situation which exists in practice. The contemplative mode of apperception produces an ideal which it identifies with the actual. It hopes for the ideal, but does not intend it in practice. Instead, it asserts that the ideal is the necessary outcome of the conflict of the actual world. To try to improve it by planning would be a dangerous interference with the natural laws which in their own good time will inevitably bring the improvement about.

These two modes of society, like the two forms of apperception which sustain them, are ambivalent expressions of the same negative motivation. Consequently, the one can transform itself into the other with ease. If the 'organic' society, idealizing its actuality, is compelled to take its practical life seriously, if the self-deception cannot be maintained any longer, then the struggle becomes real and is waged in earnest. When this happens, the unity of the society can only be maintained by the power of the State. The necessity of social unity makes it certain that it will be so maintained. Rousseau gives place to Hobbes; idealism to realism; modern democracy to the totalitarian state.

Since both these types of society depend upon negative motivation, so that the bonds of relation between individuals which constitute them are impersonal, I have called them both societies and not communities. Because our own social tradition is, on the whole, based upon a negative apperception in one or other of the ambivalent modes, or a mixture of them, we identify society and community. Even so there are overtones of difference. Since we must proceed by contrasting these negative type-forms with the positive, it may serve us well if we distinguish between society and community, reserving the term community for such personal unities of persons as are based on a positive personal motivation. The members of a community are in communion with one another, and their association is a fellowship. And since such an association exhibits the form of the personal in its fully positive personal character, it will necessarily contain within it and be constituted by its own negative, which is society. Every community is then a society; but not every society is a community.

CHAPTER SEVEN

The Celebration of Communion

In the last chapter we used the distinction between two ambivalent modes of apperception to throw light upon two type-forms of human society. This led to a suggestion that we should use the term 'society' to refer to those forms of human association in which the bond of unity is negative or impersonal; and to reserve for the contrasted forms of association which have a positive personal relation as their bond, the term 'community'. A community then rests upon a positive apperception by its members of the relation which unites them as a group. It is a personal, not an impersonal unity of persons.

It is to the structure of community, in contrast to society, that we shall now direct our attention. But before entering upon this new topic it will be well to draw attention to an ambivalence in our discussion which may seem to some to amount to a dangerous ambiguity. We have talked of modes of apperception giving rise to modes of society. But surely, it may be said, the mode in which we apperceive a thing can only give rise to a corresponding conception, not to a modification of the thing to which we are attending. Different apperceptions of society may give rise to different ideas of what society is. Some may be false, and others true; or all may be true from a certain point of view, and none fully adequate. But society is what it is, whether our ideas of what it is are adequate or inadequate, or even false.

There is, we must admit, an element of truth in this criticism, which we must try to elicit. But to do so the criticism itself must be radically revised. As it stands, it is simply mistaken. It would be valid only if a human society were mere matter of fact. But it is not. The association of persons in a unity is constituted by practical relations; by the ways in which the associates *act* in relation to one another. A relation of agents can never be mere matter of fact. It must be matter of intention. For this reason, the conception we have of our relations to one another determines the relations themselves; and the mode of apperception which is normal in any society determines the mode of the society's existence.

This does not mean, however, that the conception may not be false, or inadequate. The truth of any conception lies in its reference to action; and therefore its verification is to be found in the action which it determines. In scientific verification, where we are dealing with matter of fact, we make an experiment, to discover whether what actually happens tallies with what we expect to happen. Whether it does or not, the intention of the experiment is achieved; for it is a theoretical intention. If, however, our intention is practical, then if the conception is false the intention will not succeed. We shall achieve a result which we did not intend. The means which we adopt will not produce the result we hoped for. But if the conception is not of matter of fact but of matter of intention, then if the conception is false, the action it determines will be self-frustrating. For in this case the intention of the action itself will be misdirected. We may, of course, fail to reach our objective because we have made a mistake about the means of its achievement. But this will be a subsidiary issue. We may, however, be successful in attaining our goal; and then we shall find that the success was only an *apparent* success; that it is not what we *really* intended, that we have been aiming at the wrong thing. The self-frustration can only be removed by changing the objective.

Now if the misconception is categorial, then it makes the action inherently self-frustrating. For the error then infects the form of action in general, and not its particular content as this or that particular action. In that case, to change the objective will not remove the frustration. For whatever objective we aim at, the attainment of it will reveal itself as only an apparent success, and the end will be found to be not what we really intended. So long as we can believe that the error lies in our choice of objective, we can try again. But this cannot continue indefinitely; the alternatives are limited. The discovery that all objectives have the same illusory character is the experience of *despair*. It is expressed in the judgment that human life is inherently meaningless and that all action is futile.

A categorial misconception is a misconception of one's own nature. Error in theory involves failure in practice. This is the principle on which all verification rests. If, however, the error lies in our conception of our own nature, it must affect all our action, for we shall misconceive our own reality by appearing to ourselves to be what we are not, or not to be what we are. The result can only be a self-frustration based upon a self-deception. Under these conditions, Kant's conclusion is correct. We know ourselves only as we appear to ourselves and not as we really are. This expresses itself in action as self-frustration. Our actions appear to be determined, though they really are free. But this is only true in virtue of a negative motivation in relation to other persons. For then action is defensive and appears to be dictated by the other person, against whom I must defend myself. In reality it is determined not by him but by my fear of him. Thus, when two friends quarrel and are estranged, each blames the other for the bad relations between them. Or, to put it otherwise, if my motivation is negative then I appear to myself as an isolated individual who must act for himself and achieve whatever he can achieve by his individual efforts, in a world which cares nothing for his success or failure. Yet in reality, my isolation is a self-isolation, a withdrawal from relationships through fear of the other. This attitude, which expresses the experience of frustration and despair, is nothing but the sophisticated adult version of the attitude of the child whose mother refuses to give him what he wants. Its unsophisticated formula is, 'Nobody loves me.'

It may serve us best if we adopt, for the moment, the unsophisticated form of expression, even if it is not very precise in statement. I need you to be myself. This need is for a fully positive personal relation in which, because we trust one another, we can think and feel and act together. Only in such a relation can we really be ourselves. If we quarrel, each of us withdraws from the other into himself, and the trust is replaced by fear. We can no longer be ourselves in relation to one another. We are in conflict, and each of us loses his freedom and must act under constraint. There are two ways in which this situation can be met without actually breaking the relationship—which, we are assuming, is a necessary one. There may be a reconciliation which restores the original confidence; the negative motivation may be overcome and the positive relation re-established. Or we may agree to co-operate on conditions which impose a restraint upon each of us, and which prevent the outbreak of active hostility. The negative motivation, the fear of the other, will remain, but will be suppressed. This will make possible co-operation for such ends as each of us has an interest in achieving. But we will remain isolated individuals, and the co-operation between us, though it may appear to satisfy our need of one another, will not really satisfy *us*. For what we really need is to care for one another, and we are only caring for ourselves. We have achieved society, but not community. We have become associates, but not friends.

That the two types of society we discussed in the last chapter are not communities is clear. The categories of apperception which dictate their forms—pragmatic and contemplative alike —are expressions of a negative motivation. The Hobbesian society is based on force; Rousseau's on consent: but both are aimed only at the protection of the individual associates in the pursuit of their private interests. The debate between the two types of society concerns their efficiency for this purpose. In Hobbes this is stated explicitly: in Rousseau it is normally concealed. Yet in his formulation of the problems of a free society it is quite evident. What is required, he says, is 'a form of association which will protect . . . the person and goods of each associate'. Both forms are for the sake of protection and presuppose fear. A community is for the sake of friendship and presupposes love. But it is only in friendship that persons are free in relation; if the relation is based on fear we are constrained in it and not free. Society is maintained by a common constraint, that is to say by acting in obedience to law. This secures an appearance of freedom, for it secures me from the expression of the other's animosity. But it does so by suppression of the motive which constitutes the relation. In the last analysis this law is a moral law which I impose upon myself. The constraint is then self-constraint, which achieves a negative freedom through self-suppression. If the negative motive is presupposed, then I must put up with the paradox that I am only free when I act not freely but under obligation; not from inclination, but from duty.

In *The Self as Agent*, when we considered the forms of reflective activity, we were compelled to postpone any discussion of religion. The reason we gave was that religion cannot be understood from the standpoint of the isolated agent, but only when we are considering persons in relation. We are now at the point where this omission can be remedied. For we have now collected all the material which is necessary to enable us to understand the nature of religious experience, and so to define religion as a mode of personal experience. Until we understand what religion is we are in no position to ask whether it is valid or not, or how, if at all, its claims can be verified. We are concerned, therefore, with religion as a form of reflective activity, and with its origin in the structure of universal human experience. We are not concerned with its particular expressions in this religion or that, but with religion as such, as something people do, as a human activity.

It must have struck some readers, when we considered the personal life of the child in the family, that our description of it was full of the echoes of religious phrases with which we are familiar. It would seem that our study of infancy serves to strengthen the view of religion which has been made popular by

Freud, though it is of older origin, that it is a product of childish phantasy—the symbolic expression of a repressed wish in the adult to escape from the responsibilities and the frustrations of mature life and return to the irresponsible dependence of childhood. Religion would then be phantasy and illusion, the projection upon the universe of the father or the mother image. We might notice, in this connection, that positivist atheism, as we find it in Comte or Marx, is of the same type; though since positivism is based upon a sociological analysis it refers religion to the childhood of the race rather than of the individual. It would hardly be an overstatement to say that modern atheism, whether in communism or in liberal humanism, has its theoretical basis in this argument. The more we grow up, and the more rational we become, the more we are able to lay aside childish phantasies and to treat religion as a mythology which has outlived its usefulness. The psychological and the sociological roots of this view are present together in Rousseau, who combines a sentimental reverence for the child with a glorification of the noble savage. From this it might be argued that as we outgrow the sentimentality of the Romantic movement, we must also outgrow the sentimentality of the social theory which has its roots in Rousseau, and with it the practice of liberal democracy. Subtract the romantic sentiment from idealistic democracy and what is left is communist totalitarianism.

What then are we to say of this argument, and its conclusion that religion is an illusion? Simply that the argument is an illusory argument of a kind that we have already had several occasions to reject. It is an argument which draws a philosophical conclusion from scientific premises. It rests upon the *a priori* analogical interpretation of personal experience through biological concepts. It assumes that we become rational in the process of growing up, and that the more rational we become the more we grow out of our childish phantasies. So the further society evolves the more rational it becomes; the more mature the human race becomes the more the superstitions and mythologies of primitive life fade out. We have shown already that there is no empirical basis for this type of belief. It is, indeed, the characteristic myth of the twentieth century. Our superstitious belief that society is—or ought to be—organic, is itself a wish for the irresponsibility of the primitive. For it is primitive society which is as nearly organic in form as a human society can be, and social development moves away from the organic type— the ideal zero of human association. The more society becomes civilized, the more artificial it is; that is to say, the more it depends upon the artifices of a practical rationality. The institutions by which society maintains itself are not natural; they are artifacts, and they are maintained by effort in order to sustain the personal life of men and women, and to prevent a relapse into the barbarism of a nearly organic life. Of these institutions the family is the most primitive, the most persistent and the most fundamental.

Marx's criticism of religion, which, he himself insists, is the beginning to all social criticism, is almost grotesquely unscientific and *a priori*. Religion is a device, he thinks, for taking men's minds off their present miseries by the promise of a better life in a better world. It diverts their attention from this life to another and attaches their hopes to a world beyond. So they are reconciled to their present lot, and discouraged from any attempt to better it. It is 'opium for the people'; a promise of 'pie in the sky when you die'. It is the popular, and therefore the effective form of idealism. How did he arrive at this theory? Was it by a careful, objective study of the great variety of religions or the complex phenomena of religious experience in its most typical forms? There is no record of such study. When this hypothesis formed itself in his mind, did he seek to verify it by finding whether it would square with all the available evidence? Obviously not. If he had, he would surely have asked himself whether it accounted for the religion of his own Jewish ancestors as it is expressed in the Old Testament literature. This would have been enough to disprove the hypothesis, or at least to require a drastic revision. For that religion at least is not idealistic in Marx's sense, but materialist. It shows no interest in any other world, but is entirely concerned with the right way to maintain a human community in this world. That some expressions of some form of religion are liable to his criticism I see every reason to believe; perhaps even it may hold generally of official Christianity in Western Europe in modern times. That would provide good ground for demanding a religious reform. But to make it the basis of a theory of religion as such, even of a purely objective and scientific theory, is most unscientific. And in abstaining from a critical examination of the facts and from an attempt to verify its generalization, such a theory of religion surely betrays its origin in a subjective and emotional reaction, probably dating from early years. Such atheism, indeed, strongly suggests the projection of a childish phantasy upon the universe.

Freud's view has much more to say for itself. Its primary assertion that religion is a projection of the child's experience of family life must, it seems, be accepted; though the term 'projection' is a metaphor with misleading associations. Our own account of the relation of mother and child and its development supports it strongly. But Freud's argument concludes that religion is therefore illusory, and this is a complete *non-sequitur*. To prove this it would be necessary to show that religion as such —that is to say, its form, and not its content—is the product of phantasy. We have seen that the form of the child's experience is dependence on a personal Other; and that this form of experience is never outgrown, but provides the ground plan of all personal experience, which is constituted from start to finish by relation to the Other and communication with the Other. It is this form which finds expression in religion, no doubt; but there is nothing illusory about this. The adult who endeavours to create or to discover, in the context of mature experience, the form of positive personal relationship which he experienced as a child, is not indulging in phantasy, but seeking to realize his own nature as a person. Phantasy, as Freud recognizes, is the result of a failure to grow up properly. It is, we have seen, the result of a failure to overcome the negative phase in the rhythm of withdrawal and return. The craving for the earlier expressions of the love-relation is suppressed, and not abandoned. The result is a negative relation to the Other, a fear and hostility which must be suppressed. For if it were not suppressed, it would actively seek the destruction of the Other. The wish to destroy the father and take his place is one of the common phantasies of childhood. Would it not be as good an argument as Freud's, then, if we were to conclude that adult atheism was the projection upon the universe of *this* childish phantasy.

The fact is that Freud's argument proves too much—so much indeed that it refutes itself. It would prove, if it were valid, that all the forms of reflection, art and science, as well as religion, were projections or 'rationalizations' of childish phantasies, and therefore illusory. All reflective activities have their psychological origin in the development of phantasy in the child. This is why the negative phase of withdrawal into the self is necessary to personal development. Any of these forms of reflection may be given an illusory content. Astrology is an illusory science, astronomy a genuine one. There is plenty of illusory religion; but that does not prove that religion is illusory. Freud's argument, then, shows not that religion is illusory, but simply that he believes in science but not in religion. The most likely reason for this, since Freud is a fearless and independent thinker, is that the data for his theory of religion lie in the study of abnormal human behaviour. The religious ideas of a neurotic will naturally be the expressions of his neurosis, and as illusory as the childish fancies from which they derive.

The family is the original human community and the basis as well as the origin of all subsequent communities. It is therefore the norm of all community, so that any community is a brotherhood. So far, then, as religion is a 'projection' of the family ideal upon the larger societies of adult life, or even upon human society as a whole, there is nothing illusory or fantastical about it. The more a society approximates to the family pattern, the more it realizes itself as a community or, as Marx called it, a *truly human* society. What is both illusory and fantastic is the attempt to achieve it on the Hobbesian principle of the State as absolute power, in the hope that the State will then vanish away and leave the completely organic society of Rousseau's romantic phantasy. What is characteristic of the family is that it is neither established by force nor maintained by a sense of duty. It is established and maintained by natural affection; by a positive motive in its members. They care for one another sufficiently to have no need to fear one another. The normal positive motivation is usually sufficient to dominate the negative motives of self-interest and individualism.

Any theory of religion which is to deserve serious attention must recognize and account for certain general facts. The first is the universality of religion in human society. No human society, from the most primitive to the most completely civilized, has ever existed without a religion of some kind. This can only signify that the source of religion must lie in some characteristic of human experience which is common and universal. Secondly, though it is easy to find analogues of all other aspects of cultural activity—artistic, technological or social—there is no analogue of religion in even the highest forms of animal life. This must mean that the universal, common root of religion in human experience is definitely personal. Religion is bound up with that in our experience which makes us persons and not mere organisms. Thirdly, religion has been, as a matter of historical fact, the matrix from which all the various aspects of culture and civilization have crystallized. In primitive society religion is the sole representative of human reflection, and contains, as it were in solution, science and philosophy, Church and State, law, both moral and political, and art in all its forms. In the course of social development these have gained first a distinguishable form and finally a practical autonomy. Fourthly, religion is, in intention, inclusive of all members of the society to which it refers, and depends on their active co-operation to constitute it. Tribal religion requires that every member of the tribe should share in the religious practice of the tribe, as a condition of membership. A universal religion is for every member of the

Margin annotations:
1) universality
2) no analogue among animals
3) the matrix from which all aspects of culture & civilization crystallize
?
4) inclusive of all members of the society.

human race. A modern national religion, after the very recent and still precarious achievement of religious toleration, aims at including every member of the nation. If they no longer *must* be members, they *ought* to be. In this sense religion is characteristically inclusive and universal, unlike art and science, which *But, Judaism.* require in their practitioners special talents and special qualifications.

These four characteristics of religion are *prima facie* distinguishing characteristics of its form. Any theory of religion which neglects them or fails to account for them is *ipso facto* either inadequate or erroneous. In the light of our present study these characteristics, taken together, suggest that religion must be concerned with the original and basic formal problem of human existence, and this is the relation of persons. Since religion is certainly a reflective activity, this must mean, if it is true, that religion has its ground and origin in the problematic of the relation of persons, and reflects that problem. In that case religion is about the community of persons. We must then explore this possibility.

Any community of persons, as distinct from a mere society, is a group of individuals united in a common life, the motivation of which is positive. Like a society, a community is a group which acts together; but unlike a mere society its members are in communion with one another; they constitute a fellowship. A society whose members act together without forming a fellowship can only be constituted by a common purpose. They co-operate to achieve a purpose which each of them, in his own interest, desires to achieve, and which can only be achieved by co-operation. The relations of its members are functional; each plays his allotted part in the achievement of the common end. The society then has an organic form: it is an organization of functions; and each member is a function of the group. A community, however, is a unity of persons as persons. It cannot be defined in functional terms, by relation to a common purpose. It is not organic in structure, and cannot be constituted or maintained by organization, but only by the motives which sustain the personal relations of its members. It is constituted and maintained by a mutual affection. This can only mean that each member of the group is in positive personal relation to each of the others taken severally. The structure of a community is the nexus or network of the active relations of friendship between all possible pairs of its members.

If, then, we isolate one pair, as the unit of personal community, we can discover the basic structure of community as such. The relation between them is positively motived in each. Each, then, is heterocentric; the centre of interest and attention is in the other, not in himself. For each, therefore, it is the other who is important, not himself. The other is the centre of value. For himself he has no value in himself, but only for the other; consequently he cares for himself only for the sake of the other. But this is mutual; the other cares for him disinterestedly in return. Each, that is to say, acts, and therefore thinks and feels for the other, and not for himself. But because the positive motive contains and subordinates its negative, their unity is no fusion of selves, neither is it a functional unity of differences—neither an organic nor a mechanical unity—it is a unity of persons. Each remains a distinct individual; the other remains really other. Each realizes himself in and through the other.

Such a positive unity of persons is the self-realization of the personal. For, firstly, they are then related *as equals*. This does not mean that they have, as matter of fact, equal abilities, equal rights, equal functions or any other kind of *de facto* equality. The equality is intentional: it is an aspect of the mutuality of the relation. If it were not an equal relation, the motivation would be negative; a relation in which one was using the other as a means to his own end. Secondly, they both realize their freedom as agents, since in the absence of the fear for the self there is no constraint on either, and each can be himself fully; neither is under obligation to act a part. Thus equality and freedom are constitutive of community; and the democratic slogan, 'Liberty, equality, fraternity', is an adequate definition of community—of the self-realization of persons in relation.

We must remember, however, that to obtain this analysis we isolated two persons from their relation to all others. If their relation to one another is exclusive of the others, then its motivation in relation to the others is negative; the two friends must defend themselves against the intrusion of the rest. Their friendship becomes a positive element in a motivation which is dominantly negative and this will destroy the realization of the exclusive relation itself. To be fully positive, therefore, the relation must be in principle inclusive, and without limits. Only so can it constitute a community of persons. The self-realization of any individual person is only fully achieved if he is positively motived towards every other person with whom he is in relation. We can therefore formulate the inherent ideal of the personal. It is a universal community of persons in which each cares for all the others and no one for himself. This ideal of the personal is also the condition of freedom—that is, of a full realization of his capacity to act—for every person. Short of this there is un-integrated, and therefore suppressed, negative motivation; there is unresolved fear; and fear inhibits action and destroys freedom.

But this is nothing new, you may say, even if it is expressed in oddly abstract and new-fangled verbiage. It is just what all the universal religions have always said in simpler and more comprehensible terms. If that is so, and I see no reason to deny it—since it is not novelty but truth which we are seeking—it so far supports our hypothesis that religion is about community, and that we have been following the inherent logic of the development of religion from primitive times. We must, however, remind ourselves that any actual religion is the religion of an actual group of persons; and that the community of any actual group is highly problematical. We must relate this ideal, therefore, to the problem of personal relations in actual societies.

Consider first a primitive tribal religion. This choice has the same advantage which we found in the child's experience of relatedness in an earlier phase of our discussion. It enables us to consider a form of religious behaviour that is remote from our own, and we are not then so likely to take our own experience of religion as normal for it. Let us ask, 'What is it in primitive experience which makes these people behave in such odd religious ways? What function in their life as a community does religion have?' Now a primitive tribe is a group of people who live a common life. This is matter of fact. But we have seen that any group of persons living a common life is not fully described as matter of fact. Its unity is a matter of intention. Each member of it not merely is a member, but also intends his membership. The reflective aspect of this is that he not merely is a member, but knows that he is a member. In virtue of this knowledge he can act in association with the others either willingly or against his will; he can be either for the community or against it. The unity of any community of persons is constituted and maintained by the will to community in its members.

Idealist philosophy accepts an aspect of this in its insistence upon self-consciousness as the characteristic which distinguishes us from the animals and so differentiates a human society from an animal group. This may be a convenient point, therefore, at which to say the little that requires to be said about self-consciousness. We may notice first that it fails to provide a distinction between society and community. For the self-conscious individual, though he then knows that he is a member of the group, is not thereby committed to willing his membership, but merely to recognizing it. He has still to decide whether to leave the group or to remain in it for reasons of self-interest, or to maintain it as a community by action which cares for the others rather than himself.

Secondly, self-consciousness is not primary but secondary; not a positive but a negative aspect of the personal relation. My primary knowledge is knowledge of the Other. But if the Other is a person, I know him as another agent. The primary problematic of the relation is whether he is for me or against me. But an agent is also a subject; and in knowing him as an agent I know him as a subject for whom I am an object. Now if I am in full fellowship with him, if there is no constraint in the relationship, my consciousness is centred upon him and my interest and attention have the other as their focus. If, however, a constraint lies upon me in the relation, I fear his hostility, and am to that extent thrown on the defensive against him. The reflective aspect of this is that I become self-conscious. I become conscious of myself as an object which he may value negatively, as an object of possible hostile criticism. He may judge me inferior, beneath his notice, and I must be ready to justify myself in his eyes. This explains why, in ordinary speech, self-consciousness is a synonym for shyness. We may say then that self-consciousness is potential in the relation of persons at all times, but becomes actual only when there is a failure of freedom in the relation, so that it has to be maintained by an effort of will.

In any actual community of persons, then, there is not merely a common life, but also a consciousness of the common life, and it is this consciousness which constitutes the association a personal association or community. But all personal consciousness is problematic; so that the consciousness of the common life is *ipso facto* a consciousness that it may or may not be realized in action. It is the consciousness that hostility may take the place of fellowship, and the unity be broken. This will happen if personal relations become negatively motived, if fear of the others replaces love for the others. Thus the problem of community is the problem of overcoming fear and subordinating the negative to the positive in the motivation of persons in relation.

This problem, as we recognized earlier, is the basic problem of all personal life. The whole problematic of the personal has its origin here, in whatever aspect it may present itself under particular circumstances or from a particular point of view. All other problems are contained in the problem of maintaining the network of positive personal relationship which constitutes a human community. If we remember that we are not talking of an object but of the living of a personal life in common, we may say that any human group is a community in so far as its normal apperception is communal, and is determined, as to its form, by a positive category.

THE CELEBRATION OF COMMUNION

The primary form of reflection, then, will be the reflection of this problem; and since this problem is the root of the whole problematic of the personal, this form of reflection will be the matrix of all forms of reflection, and will contain them, as it were, in solution. It will also be both universal in its occurrence, and inclusive in its scope. These, however, are precisely the characteristics that we assigned to religion; and if we now say that religion is the form of reflection which relates to the problematic of community, our definition of religion will meet the requirements for a theory of religion which can be taken seriously. It explains the empirical characters that are the *differentiae* of religion as such. We must define it by its positive character, and then recognize the negative which it contains and subordinates. We must, that is to say, define it as the reflection of actual community, and not merely of the unrealized intention of community. Religion, we shall say, is the reflective activity which expresses the consciousness of community; or more tersely, religion is the celebration of communion.

To celebrate anything is to do something which expresses symbolically our consciousness of it and our joy in being conscious of it. To celebrate communion or fellowship must then involve a communal reflection, in which all members of the community share. It must find its expression in a common activity which has a symbolic character, with a reference beyond itself; an activity undertaken not for its own sake but for the sake of what it means or signifies. The celebration of communion cannot be solitary or private reflection: it must be a common activity. The members of a primitive community do in fact live a common life; but they also perform in common certain ritual activities which express their consciousness that they live a common life and their joy in the knowledge. This celebration of their fellowship is their religious activity; and since it symbolizes or expresses their common consciousness of the community life, such activity is an activity of reflection. We are reminded here that the distinction between action and reflection is not a distinction between 'material' and 'mental'

162

activity, but lies in the intention of the activity. Reflective activity is symbolic, and refers beyond itself for its meaning.

But now we must recognize the negative within this positive definition. The continuous possibility that hostility and enmity may break out between members of the community and destroy the fellowship is inseparable from any consciousness of it. For community is matter of intention and therefore problematical. What is celebrated is not a fact, but an achievement; and the community has to be maintained in the future. Moreover, the community so far achieved is imperfect, and contains not merely the possibility but also the evidences of failure. In face of this problem, religion is itself intentional. Its celebration of communion is also a means of strengthening the will to community. The function of religion is then to mobilize and strengthen the positive elements in the motivation of its members, to overcome the negative motives where they exist, to prevent the outbreak of enmity and strife, to dominate the fear of the Other and subordinate the centrifugal to the centripetal tendencies in the community. If then we take into account the development of society from the small, primitive family or kinship group to an ever greater inclusiveness, which in our own time is approaching universality, we may define the function of religion as being to create, maintain and deepen the community of persons and to extend it without limit, by the transformation of negative motives and by eliminating the dominance of fear in human relations. To achieve this would be to create a universal community of persons in which all personal relations were positively motived, and all its members were free and equal in relation. Such a community would be the full self-realization of the personal.

The individual members of a community must, however, know the significance of the religious ritual in which they participate, for if not, it can have no significance. How then can the individual represent to himself the meaning of any religious symbolism? The formal problem of this representation lies in the representation of community itself. For what has to be represented is a relation to a personal Other; and this representation must be the same for all members of the community if it is to be valid. How can a universal mutuality of intentional and active relationship be represented symbolically? Only through the idea of a personal Other who stands in the same mutual relation to every member of the community. Without the idea of such a universal and personal Other it is impossible to represent the unity of a community of persons, each in personal fellowship with all the others. This may seem to go too far unless we remember that all the members are persons, that each is an agent, and that this unity is a unity of action. The universal Other must be represented as a universal Agent, whose action unifies the actions of every member of the community, and whose continuing intention is the unity of all their several intentions. One aspect of this necessity is the need that any community has for a person as its head; a father who is the head of the family, a king or a president or a chief. The necessity is not primarily for a ruler, but for a ritual head, a representative of the unity of the community as a personal reality, so that each member can think his membership of the community through his relation to this person, who represents and embodies the intention which constitutes the general fellowship.

In its full development, the idea of a universal personal Other is the idea of God. There is an inherent logical necessity in this development. The ritual head of an existing family or kinship group is inadequate as a representation of the community. For the community has a history which links it with the past, and this continuity with the past cannot be represented by any existing member of the group. The chief is only the temporary representative of the tribal community, himself related to the representative of a unity which spans the generations. The universal Other must thus be at least the original and originating head of the community, the original father of the kinship group. This explains the development of religion as ancestor-worship. But there is another kind of limitation to be noticed. The common life, which is a life of co-operative action, is realized only through the means of life—which in general is the non-personal aspect of the world, and just as the individual must contrast himself with the community to which he belongs, so the community as a whole must contrast itself with the world to which it belongs, recognizing itself as part of the whole world of existence. The fear of the Other is, at bottom, the fear of life; and this has two aspects, which are ultimately one—it is the fear of other people and the fear of Nature. Death is at once our defeat at the hand of the forces of nature and our final isolation from the community of the living. The representation of the community as a personal unity must then have two aspects—the first developing as ancestor-worship, the other as Nature-worship, and the function of religion is as much to transform the fear of Nature as the fear of one's fellows; to achieve the dominance of the positive over the negative in the motivation of action, to whatever aspect of experience the negative motive is directed, and from whatever source its dominance in human behaviour is derived. For this reason religious reflection, when it is full-grown, must represent the original personal author of the community as the author of the world; and the life of community as a fellowship of the world—of man with Nature as well as of man with man. Or rather, it must represent the personal community as maintained through an organic harmony between man and the world. The personal must include and subordinate the non-personal for the sake of the realization of the personal.

If this basic problem of personal life could be resolved, if the negative motive could finally and completely be subordinated to the positive, in all personal activity, the redemptive function of religion would be complete; and only its central activity would remain. Religion would then be simply the celebration of communion—of the fellowship of all things in God. Meanwhile, it sustains the intention to achieve this fellowship.

CHAPTER EIGHT

Reflection and the Future

Action is the determination of the future. Freedom is the capacity to act, and so the capacity to determine the future. This freedom has two dimensions; the capacity to move, and the capacity to know; both of which have reference to the Other. To move is to modify the Other: to know is to apprehend the Other. To act, then, as the essential unity of these two freedoms is to modify the Other by intention.[1] To this we add that since the agent is part of the Other, he cannot modify the Other without modifying himself, or know the Other without knowing himself. In determining the future for the Other he also determines his own future. Self-determination is thus included in action as a negative aspect. It is negative because the intention is directed upon the Other, not upon oneself.

The freedom of any particular agent, however, depends upon his knowledge of the Other, and this knowledge is problematic. So far as his knowledge of the Other is infected with error, his capacity to act will be frustrated; his intention will not be realized. This frustration does not mean that he cannot act at all, but that he will act wrongly and the resulting determination of the future will not be what he intended, and hence not in the strict sense *his* determination. It will be determined for him through his own act in a way which he did not intend. This must include, of course, a self-determination which is unintentional. Again, his freedom of action will depend upon the

[1] Cf. *The Self as Agent*, Chap. VI.

adequacy of his knowledge: he will be able to determine the future only to the extent of his knowledge, even if it is valid so far as it goes.

The reflective activities of the personal are, therefore, concerned with the development of knowledge, and this development has two interrelated aspects, eliminating error and enlarging its scope. The development of knowledge is primarily concerned with our knowledge of the Other; but this will include, as its negative, knowledge of ourselves. The reflective activities, as negative aspects of action, are for the sake of action; they are symbolic actions, as it were, with a meaning; and this meaning is a reference beyond the symbols to what they signify. In general, this reference is from reflection to action; from a symbolic or imaginary action to real action. Now since action is the determination of the future, all reflective activities have a reference to the future and its determination. They determine the future symbolically, but not in reality.

We have determined three forms of reflection—religion, art and science. It remains for us to consider their relation to the future and to one another. It will help us in this task if we remember that all must be concerned with the extension of knowledge and the elimination of error; and so with creating the conditions of freedom, that is to say, of action as the capacity to determine the future in accordance with an intention. Further, since it is the capacity to act—to do something knowing what we are doing—that makes us persons, and since reason is the traditional term which we apply to the *differentia* of the personal, the forms of reflection will be modes of rationality.

The primary mode of reflective rationality, then, is religion. It is, as we have seen, primary in the historical and genetic sense. It is both the first form of reflection to manifest itself in human development, and the matrix from which the other forms are historically derived. But it is also, as we shall see, the primary mode analytically. It is the basic mode with which the others must function if they are to maintain their own rationality. We shall therefore consider religion first of all, and seek to discover the logical derivation of art and science from it, as forms of reflective rationality.

Religion, as a mode of reflection, is concerned with the knowledge of the personal Other. The data for such reflection are our experiences of personal relationship. We know other persons, in our practical activities, by entering into personal relation with them. Reflection, however, being derivative, can arise only from a problem set by failure in action. Religious reflection, therefore, arises from a failure in personal relationship, and its reference, as a symbolic activity, is to personal relationship. It aims at knowledge of the personal Other in mutual relation with oneself; it is for the sake of the life of active personal relationship; its function is, therefore, to understand the reason for the failure so that the relationship may be resumed in a way that will avoid failure in future.

Now any form of reflection universalizes its problem, however particular it may be in origin. The withdrawal from action is a withdrawal from the particularity of a situation; and the substitution of a symbol for the particular reality has the effect of universalization. For the symbolic resolution of the problem will apply to all cases to which the symbols can refer. This is quite independent of any immediate interest. If I reflect upon the reason why a particular friend has taken offence at something I have done, I may have no other interest than to discover how to restore the relation between us. But if I do reach an understanding, I have improved my knowledge of personal relationship in general, and can avoid this sort of mistake with other people. Religious knowledge, therefore, universalizes the problem of personal relationship, and seeks an understanding of personal relationship as such. We must not confuse this universality with mere generalization, which is characteristic of scientific reflection. Each form of reflection has its own type of universality. Art does not generalize; on the contrary, it particularizes; yet its insight is universal in its own mode. Religious reflection, for reasons we have already touched upon, universalizes its problem through the idea of a universal Person to whom all particular agents stand in an identical relation. This is the idea of God, and religious knowledge is rightly described as the knowledge of God. Such knowledge will apply universally to all instances of personal relationship.

The form of religious reflection is necessarily determined by its data; and these are our practical experiences of our relations with one another. How then do we know one another, and what form does this knowledge take? Clearly, it has a very different form from our knowledge of the material world. It is not, and cannot be, objective or scientific. A purely objective attitude to another person precludes a personal knowledge, because it excludes direct personal relationship. We can know a great deal about other people, both in particular and in general, without knowing them. The reason for this is simply the mutuality of the personal. If I know you, then it follows logically that you know me. If you do not know me, then necessarily I do not know you. To know another person we must be in communication with him, and communication is a two-way process. To be in communication is to have something in common. Knowledge of other people is simply the negative or reflective aspect of our personal relations with them.

From this there follows an interesting corollary. All knowledge of persons is by revelation. My knowledge of you depends not merely on what I do, but upon what you do; and if you refuse to reveal yourself to me, I cannot know you, however much I may wish to do so. If in your relations with me, you consistently 'put on an act' or 'play a role', you hide yourself from me. I can never know you as you really are. In that case, generalization from the observed facts will be positively misleading. This puts the scientific form of knowledge out of court in this field. For scientific method is based on the assumption that things are what they appear to be; that their behaviour necessarily expresses their nature. But a being who can pretend to be what he is not, to think what he does not think, and to feel what he does not feel, cannot be known by generalization from his observed behaviour, but only as he genuinely reveals himself.

But we must go deeper than this. The 'I' and the 'You', we have said, are constituted by their relation. Consequently, I know myself only as I reveal myself to you; and you know yourself only in revealing yourself to me. Thus, self-revelation is at the same time self-discovery. This may sound paradoxical, yet it is a commonplace of personal experience. In no field of knowledge is anything really known until it is expressed; and to express knowledge is to put it in the form of a communication. In the personal field this is merely complicated by the mutuality of the personal relation. One can only really know one's friends, and oneself through one's friends, in a mutuality of self-revelation. This self-revelation is, of course, primarily practical, and only secondarily a matter of talk. We sometimes call it 'giving oneself away', and contrast it with 'keeping oneself to oneself'.

Now because of this such knowledge of another person as we can achieve depends upon our emotional disposition towards him. In the formal terms of our earlier analysis, a negative personal relation between persons makes knowledge of the other and of oneself alike impossible. For mutual dislike or hostility inhibits self-revelation. Of course, I still form an 'idea' of my enemy; and I shall take my representation of him to be the truth. But this will necessarily be an illusion. I shall know him as he appears to be, but not as he really is; and the knowledge will be 'unreal'. My knowledge of another person is a function of my love for him; and in proportion as my knowledge is a function of my fear of him, it is illusory or unreal. The problematic of our knowledge of persons is in terms of the distinction between reality and illusion, between 'real' and 'unreal'.

The problematic of religion, therefore, is in terms of this distinction. Religion itself, in any of its manifestations, can be real or illusory. The distinction rests upon the motivation which sustains religious reflection. If the motivation is negative the religious activity and the knowledge which informs it will be illusory; it will be real so far as it is positively motived. Illusory religion is, then, egocentric, for the sake of oneself, defensive; it is grounded in the fear of life. Real religion is heterocentric. So far as it is concerned with oneself, it is for the sake of the other. All religion, as we have seen, is concerned to overcome fear. We can distinguish real religion from unreal by contrasting their formulae for dealing with negative motivation. The maxim of illusory religion runs: 'Fear not; trust in God and He will see that none of the things you fear will happen to you'; that of real religion, on the contrary, is 'Fear not; the things that you are afraid of are quite likely to happen to you, but they are nothing to be afraid of.'

We have been considering religion from the point of view of the individual. If we look at it from the point of view of the society whose religion it is, we can express this in terms of the categories of apperception. Any society of persons, united in a common life, has a religious aspect. Atheism, if it is in action, is an effort to suppress this aspect; if it is passive, it is a failure to recognize it. Both active and passive atheism are normally reactions against unreal religion, and even so they are accidental and unusual. All societies therefore have religions which express and symbolize their consciousness of community. But if their normal apperception is negative the religion will be unreal. If the apperception is pragmatic, the religion will have the form, as it were, of a spiritual technology; an armoury of devices to control the forces which determine practical success or failure, but which are beyond the reach of ordinary human power; a set of ritual devices which placate the hostility or enlist the favour of the divine. If the apperception is contemplative, the religion will be idealist or 'purely spiritual'. Such religion tends in various manners to be 'otherworldly', for it is characteristically the representation of an ideal community which is hoped for and imagined, but not intended in practice. It is a withdrawal from the world; an escape into phantasy: it refers its symbols not to the common world of actual life, but away from it to another world which compensates for the unsatisfactory character of the actual. It tends, therefore, to make central a belief in the immortality of the soul, and like all idealism, to invert the relation between reality and appearance. It makes the spiritual world real; the material world unreal and illusory.

The problematic of religion, then, is in terms of the distinction between reality and unreality in the relation of persons. For this reason the primary demand of religion is for a personal integrity. Integrity here is not a general term for moral goodness: it means specifically a way of life which is integral. In particular, an integration of the inner life with the outer, a unity of reflection and action, a coincidence of motive and intention. If this were complied with, the result would be action which is at once moral and spontaneous, and consequently, free. The opposite of this is action which is 'hypocritical' in its etymological sense of 'play-acting', or 'acting a part', 'sustaining a role'. Integrity, then, is incompatible with dualism in any form and religion is therefore incompatible with acquiescence in dualism, whether in its pragmatic or its idealist mode.

We should notice that it is acquiescence in dualism that is the real issue, not the fact of dualism. Religion expresses the intention to realize integrity, in the face of the dualism that pervades the personal world. If dualism were not the fact, if there were no unreality in personal life, then there would be no need for religion, and religion would never make its appearance. But if we acquiesce in dualism, there is no point in religion, and religion itself becomes a sentimentality. To suppress religion is, therefore, to suppress the consciousness of unreality in ourselves, and, in Rousseau's phrase, to 'take men as they are, and States as they ought to be'. This is to project our unreality upon the impersonal Other, denying it in ourselves. It is this self-deception which religion refuses. It recognizes the constraint of necessity which maintains the unity of social co-operation, whether as an external compulsion or an inner repression; whether as a law enforced by the Other or as a law which we impose upon ourselves. But for religion it is the necessity of this constraint that is the problem of problems—the problem of evil. The problem is, 'Why can we not do as we please?' The negative modes of morality give a reason; and the form of their argument is, 'Because it is in the nature of things that we should not.' Religion rejects this answer; its own has another form. 'Why not, indeed? The fact that we cannot is the problem. Let us discover what is wrong and put it right.'

Now, since religion is a form of reflection, it is a search for knowledge, that is, for a valid symbolic representation. But because its problematic is in terms of the distinction of real and unreal the question to be asked about its representation is not simply whether it is true, nor merely whether it is satisfying, but whether it is *real*. This is a question which includes the other two questions and demands their unification. If it is true but unsatisfactory, or if is satisfactory but untrue, it is unreal. Now truth is judged; satisfaction is felt: consequently the reflection which is concerned with the problematic of truth is an intellectual reflection, while the reflection that is concerned with satisfactoriness is emotional. The first is concerned with matter of fact; the second with matter of intention, that is to say, with value. Both, as representational, refer to action and have their verification in action.

The knowledge which is involved in action has two aspects, which correspond to the reflective distinction between means and end. As knowledge of means, it is an answer to the question, 'What, as a matter of fact, is the means to a given end?'; as knowledge of ends, it is the answer to another question, 'Which, of the possible ends, is the most satisfactory end to pursue?' This second question is concerned with value, not with matter of fact. It initiates a reflective activity which seeks to arrange an order of priority between possible ends. Action itself involves the integration of these two types of knowledge. To act is to choose to realize a particular objective, in preference to all other possible objectives, by an effective means. In reflection, however, these two questions are necessarily separated, because they require two different modes of reflective activity for their solution. From this it follows that the problematic of religion, which requires their integration, can only be solved in action and not in reflection. The validity of a theological doctrine, for instance, cannot be determined merely by asking whether it is true. For this is only one aspect of its reality. Its validity depends also upon the valuation with which it is integrated in action. It is characteristic of theological doctrines that they are ambivalent in this respect. The Christian doctrine of the incarnation may mean, to one who accepts it, either that he is expected to live according to the pattern set by Christ, or that he cannot be expected to do so.

Religion, therefore, has two aspects, ritual and doctrine. The first is aesthetic in form, the second scientific. Of the two aspects, the aesthetic is the positive and primary, since it is valuational, and refers to the intention of action; the scientific is secondary and negative, since the means presupposes the end. These aspects are not, of course, science and art; the distinction has reference only to their form. As aspects of religion they are held together and complement one another—looking to their integration in action. Or, to put it otherwise, both refer to the unity of action which constitutes reality; the one to its aspect as fact, the other to its aspect as value. The one refers to an absolute Truth which is the standard of all partial truths; the other to an absolute Satisfactoriness (or Goodness) which is the standard of all partial goods. In their togetherness they symbolize the unity of Truth and Goodness. But this unity is realized only in action; so that reality is symbolized as the one action which intends the unity of Truth and Goodness, and which achieves its end with absolute efficiency. To this we must add that the problem of the unreal is the problem of the personal, and action depends upon the relation of persons. The absolute intention must, therefore, be the realization of a universal community; the means to this the actuality of the world as history. This can only be satisfactorily expressed in religious terms, as we should expect; since no form of reflection can be adequately translated into another. The language of religion, which wrestles with the problematic of the personal, is necessarily a personal language. We might say—to use a form of words with which we are familiar—that the reality of the world is a personal

God, who is the Creator of the world and the Father of all men. His work in history is the redemption of the world from evil and the setting up of the Kingdom of Heaven on earth.

If the motive which sustains a religion becomes negative, the religion itself must become unreal. In that case, the religion may either become aggressive—seeking to achieve community by force and achieving, at most, a pragmatic society; or it may become submissive, contemplative and idealistic, referring its reflective symbolism to another world; to a community which is expected but not intended. We must refrain from elaborating this theme, tempting though it is, in order to concentrate our attention upon a more urgent issue. We must consider the loosing of the ties which unite the two aspects of religion—the intellectual and the emotional—so that they enter upon an independent life of their own and become autonomous as science and art respectively.

It should be remembered in this and similar connections that when we derive the negative forms from the positive by a negation of the positive, the purpose is methodological and expository. It must not be interpreted as though it were constitutive. In the rhythm of withdrawal and return, the negative phase may be intentionally for the sake of the return; or it may not be. In the latter case the return is for the sake of the withdrawal. In the form of the personal the positive always contains and is constituted by its negative. Consequently there is no reason why both science and art should not be integrated with religion, as the two ambivalent forms of the negative which is necessary to its constitution. Indeed, the development of religion requires the discrimination of the two forms of reflection within it, if it is not to fall into illusion. If, on the other hand, any religion falls into unreality by losing its reference to the real world, that is, the world of action, art or science or both must become substitutes for religion. For the reference of reflection to action is necessary. If it is not maintained in one way it must be maintained in another. The same principle holds in all fields of personal experience. We distinguished between a positive and two negative modes of morality;[1] between community and two forms of society.[2] But the reality of community implies society in both its forms, as necessary to it, in due subordination within it. Community which does not express itself in co-operative activity for common purposes is illusory—a mere sentimentality. Similarly, the positive morality of love contains and subordinates the two negative moralities of good form and of self-control.

Art and science are derived from religion by a limitation of attention. They are activities of reflection carried on for their own sake, and not for the sake of the personal Other. The one is an activity of emotional reflection, the other of intellectual reflection. As aspects of religion they refer to action which integrates them, and they have therefore a reference to one another and qualify one another. This is possible only so far as action is positively motived and heterocentric. If they are carried on for their own sakes, the reference to the personal Other is excluded from this intention of the activity; though it necessarily remains as matter of fact. As a result they lose their intentional reference to one another and become antithetical. Religion, we might say, intends the synthesis of art and science; art and science each intend themselves and exclude one another. Art intends the determination of the possible, not of the actual. Its problematic is in terms of satisfactory or unsatisfactory, and it is therefore an activity of valuation. Science intends the determination of the actual, not of the possible. Its problematic is in terms of true or false, and it is concerned with matter of fact. Both, however, are impersonal activities, in the sense that neither intends the personal. The relation of both the artist and the scientist to the world is an impersonal relation. In the critical case, which is the relation to their fellow-men, they stay aloof. The scientist, intellectually reflective, observes, compares, generalizes and records; the artist contemplates, isolates, particularizes and evaluates, in an activity of emotional reflection.

We must not forget, however, that both art and science are,

---

[1] *Supra*, Chap. V.
[2] *Supra*, Chap. VI.

as a matter of fact, personal activities. They are the activities of persons, and only of persons. It is the relation to the Other that is impersonal. Artist and scientist alike are doing something, and the unity of the personal informs the doing. In both cases, therefore, the motive and intention are operative together; both intellectual and emotional forces are at work. There is, then, in all art an intellectual element, and in all science an emotional element. The intention, however, is in science intellectual, and therefore factual; in art it is emotional and evaluative. Formally, the artistic aspect in science is negative and subordinate, for the sake of the scientific; while in art the relation is reversed. Further, as personal activities they are forms of reflective rationality, though they are limited forms. Their rationality consists in their problematical character and their reference to the world of action for their verification. Their limitation is a limitation of this reference. Both refer only to an aspect of experience. In this sense they are abstract forms of rationality. Action based upon a valid intellectual analysis of the world may as a whole be irrational, since its intention may be evil; and action based on a valid valuation may equally be irrational as a whole; as, for example, the effort to achieve community by force.

To complete this comparison, we must add that of the two abstract forms of rationality, the aesthetic is primary, the scientific is secondary and subordinate. This follows at once from the fact that the end determines the means and not vice versa. It is, of course, possible to allow the means to determine the end. We do this whenever we exploit any sort of power for its own sake. But this is inherently irrational, or rather it can be rational only by reference to a valid intention to which it is itself the means, as when we act experimentally, testing the efficiency of a means before using it for a positive purpose. The reference in science to action is to its aspect as means; that of art is to its aspect as end; and the end includes, as a negative, the means to the end in the same way as the conclusion of a syllogism includes its premises. For this reason science is pragmatic while art is contemplative.

We discover, then, three forms of reflective rationality, of which the fully intentional expressions are religion, art and science respectively. All of these are equally rational, for reason is the same in all its manifestations. It would be an error to think that science is less rational than art or art than religion. But it is true to say that science is the lowest, religion the highest form of reflective rationality, while the rationality of art is intermediate. From the point of view of the agent, the validity of his action—its reality as action—has three aspects. The means chosen must be efficient, the end to be realized must be satisfactory, and the action as a whole must be moral, that is to say, compatible with the community of action as a whole. Of these aspects, the moral validity is primary. It is the governing condition of the full and ultimate satisfactoriness of the end. For the end achieved may be satisfactory in itself, considered abstractly in isolation. Its value may be intrinsic. Yet it may conflict with the ends of other agents which are equally valid in themselves, and in such circumstances its intrinsic validity may not justify its realization. Further, the end realized may be unsatisfactory in itself, yet the means chosen to realize it may be efficient. In that case, a valid means has been misused.

The propriety of this analysis is borne out by an examination of the structure of language, so far as it is relevant to the issue. The form of the personal is a relation of persons; and a person is an agent. To be an agent is to be in active relation with the Other, which includes himself. Thus the unit of the personal is two persons in community in relation to a common Other which includes them. The basic condition of their community is communication, and language is their normal means of communication. Language must, therefore, reflect this structure of relationships. It does so by distinguishing and symbolizing three persons, which the grammarians call the first, second and third persons. The first person is the speaker, symbolized as 'I', the second is the person addressed, the 'You', and the third is the person or thing spoken about. The fact that this last element is called a person reminds us of our conclusion that the Other is primarily personal, and that the impersonal is a discrimination within it—its negative aspect. Thus the grammarian's third person is symbolized as 'he, she or it'.

The full situation which is thus reflected is two persons in communication about a common Other. The 'I' and 'You' are talking to one another; and the mutuality of the relation is expressed by the interchange of the symbols. When I speak to you, I am the first person, you are the second. When you reply you become the first person and I the second. The symbols are interchangeable. The third person is the same for both of us, the common other about which we are talking. It is this whole situation which is generalized in religious reflection as the community of persons in active relation to the universal Other, that is, to God.

Now we can derive the situation which is reflected in art and science by successive limitations of this grammatical structure. In aesthetic reflection, we may say, the second person is intentionally excluded. The 'You' cannot, of course, be excluded as a matter of fact, for the 'I' is constituted by his relation to the 'You', but he can be excluded by a limitation of attention. The second person, excluded from attention, is not abolished, but he is not individualized. He is, as it were, treated as a negligible constant. The artist's activity is one of expression; it is not complete until its product is exhibited, or at least externalized in a form which can be exhibited, to other people. Expression implies exhibition, and exhibition implies communication. But the communication is not to another person to whom the artist stands in a personal relation. It is to a public; to anyone who has the interest to accept and the ability to understand. In the activity of reflective and symbolic representation, however, the artist's intention is not communication—that supervenes upon the completion of his task—it is limited to expression, to the construction of an adequate image.

Art then, as emotional reflection expressing itself in the construction of an adequate image, is an activity of the isolated self in mutual, but impersonal relation to the Other. Its grammatical schema includes the first and third persons, and excludes the second person. The inclusion of the first person signifies that the completed symbol expresses not the object of the artist's attention merely, but himself, as an individual person, in relation to the object. For this reason the same object will give rise to different symbols and different valuations for every artist. The expression is not of the object as such but of the artist's vision of the object.

If now we take a step farther, and exclude in intention not only the second but also the first person, we have the schema of scientific or intellectual reflection. Again, the first person cannot in fact be eliminated; he can only be generalized and treated as a negligible constant. The scientist is indeed a person, and the scientific activity is his activity. But he must intentionally exclude himself—reduce himself to a mere observer who records what happens and takes pains to see that his personal reaction to what happens is excluded from what is symbolized. The scientist must take precautions which will eliminate the personal factor, and make allowances for the errors of observation to which it may give rise. What he observes and what he symbolizes must be the same for all possible observers. What remains of the schema of communication is only the third person, isolated in intention from all relation to the personal reality of the observer, as well as from that of the persons to whom the results of his reflection may thereafter be communicated. Science is thus completely impersonal and merely objective. It knows, or at least intends to know, only the Other in its isolation. Whether this is actually possible must remain doubtful. Until recently science felt assured that it was possible to know the impersonal Other as it is in itself. But contemporary science has found reason to doubt this, and is busy revising its theory in consequence. From the philosopher's point of view this was to be expected, and makes no essential difference. Observation can take note only of what appears to the observer. Whether the relation of the object to the person observing it makes an essential difference to objective knowledge we cannot be certain, and there is no need to be certain. All that is necessary to scientific rationality is that what is observed should be the same for all possible observers. Whether this guarantees that the object is known as it is when it is not observed, known 'as it is in itself', is inherently doubtful, and indeed the question seems to be nonsensical. Can it mean anything to ask what a thing looks like when no one is looking? It is enough that this product of scientific reflection should be the same for all scientists. This guarantees its rationality. In art, on the other hand, the opposite is the case. The product of artistic reflection is necessarily different for every artist. If two painters were to produce identical representations of the same scene, the genuineness of the work of the one or of the other or of both would at once be questionable. Either one would be a copy of the other, or both mere mechanical reproductions of the scene, using the same technique but devoid of genuine emotional reflection.

The rationality of any mode of reflection lies in its reference to the Other. Without this reference reflection is mere phantasy, mere imagination. Art and science are, from one point of view at least, both objective and both equally objective. The one objectivity is descriptive, the other valuational. If art were not objective, it would have no problematic; it would be a mere subjective play of fancy. It would be impossible that there should be a distinction between good and bad art, and all products of art would be meaningless and insignificant. It is not easier to produce a great drama than to make a great scientific discovery. It is much more difficult. The possible data for art and for science are the same—the whole range of our experience of the world. Both demand an intense and impersonal concentration upon the world. Both have their interest fixed upon the other, not upon the self. Both extend our knowledge of the world, though in different fashion, and of the two kinds of knowledge it is that yielded by the insight of the artist that is more important. The denial of this rests upon the traditional dogma, which we have already dismissed, that feeling cannot be cognitive.

Now, from the standpoint of the Agent, the reference of all

reflection is to action. But action is the determination of the future. Both art and science, therefore, have a reference to the future, and this reference constitutes their rationality, and provides the means of their validation. The resolution of their problematic lies only in action, and action is concerned with the future. Reflection, we have seen, is about the past, about the existent—that which is already determinate. But it *refers* to the future. The actual is datum for science. It is the model for art. But as activities directed upon the actual, both point beyond it, to what is not yet.

The reference of science to the future is clear. Science provides that kind of knowledge which can form the basis for technology; that is to say, for the provision of techniques for the achievement of intentions. Through the scientific extension of knowledge we learn how to do what we want to do and could not do, or not so effectively, without it. Thus science increases the range of our power. But it is indifferent as regards the objectives of action. It can therefore be used for good or bad ends indifferently, to further intentions which are either rational or irrational. Science presupposes intentions and does not evaluate them. As a dimension of action, scientific knowledge is the negative aspect of technology, that is to say, of action regarded as means. For this reason the problematic of science—true or false?—is resolved by experiment. We do something which will achieve a certain result if the theory is true but not if the theory is false. This does not mean that science is necessarily carried on by scientists for the sake of technology. It may be pursued for its own sake, and is probably at its best when so pursued. But whatever the immediate aim of the scientist, knowledge always is ultimately for the sake of action. The negative is always for the sake of the positive. And the aspect of action for which science exists—its function for the community—is its technological aspect. It envisages the actual as the means of action and asks only questions to which answers can be verified experimentally, that is, by their use as the basis of a technology.

Art, on the other hand, starting from the same world of actual experience, contemplates instead of merely observing. It does not refer the object which it contemplates to a class and seek to discover and formulate a general law. Instead it isolates and individualizes its object, and seeks to penetrate beneath the surface appearance to the individual reality which makes it significant. The artist is in search not of a law, but of a form; and the concepts of 'law' and 'form' are related as the concepts of 'means' and 'end'. For a law is a rule for achieving ends: it is technological. A form is an achieved finality, to be contemplated and enjoyed. When it is referred to the future it defines a finality to be achieved, and so the unity of the action as it is intended to be; an organic unity of its elements, complete in itself and therefore satisfactory.

Form, in this sense, is always ideal. It is a standard to which the actual can only approximate. For the actual is always in process and never complete; and any object of contemplation presents a form which is due as much to the whole actual within which it exists as to its own individual being. It is the form that would express the isolated individual in its own self-realization which the artist seeks. To reproduce the form actually observed would be useless: it would be totally inadequate to the artistic aim. The observed form is only the starting-point of a reflective activity of feeling which must create an adequate form, complete in itself; with a unity achieved by the functional relation of divergent elements, and characterized by the rhythm, balance and harmony of its differences. 'Art', said Mr. Roger Fry, 'is significant form.' I prefer to express what I take to be substantially the same idea by saying that art is the expression of satisfactory form in an adequate image. The form is universal, a standard of satisfactoriness for contemplation. The image is its embodiment in a particular combination of sensible elements. Only so can form be exhibited; for a form must be the form of something; and the significance of form cannot be intellectually apprehended, it must be felt.

The function of art, then—its place in the economy of the personal, and so in action as the determination of the future—

is the education and refinement of sensibility. Sensibility is feeling determining an image, as we saw at an early stage of our discussion.[1] In action, this image is the 'image of the end', as Aristotle said, and as such the representation of the Good as a form. 'The Good', to quote Aristotle once again, 'may be defined as that at which all things aim.'[2] This capacity to envisage the future before we act and while we act is itself the form of intentionality. For in acting we must envisage our action as ideally complete and satisfactorily achieved. We refer to this as 'the formation of an intention', and this expression is satisfactory so long as we remember that the intention is itself formed in the process of acting, and the intention present before the action begins is only the germ of an intention which develops during the action and is mature only when the action is completed. Of this aspect of action art is the reflective mode.

Science, then, is knowledge of the Other as means. This knowledge it represents as a universal system of laws of Nature, which forms the theoretical basis for all possible techniques. Art is the knowledge of the Other as ends, which it represents as a set of universal forms which are the standards of satisfactoriness or value for contemplation, and therefore the basis for all satisfactory intentions. But in reflection the two aspects are unrelated and antithetical. Action is the unity of means and end: it involves a double choice—of ends to be achieved and of the means to their achievement. Science provides a knowledge of the general rules of efficiency in action without reference to the intentions to be realized through them. Art exhibits the general forms of all satisfactory achievement, that is to say, of intrinsic values, of ends which are indirectly worth achieving, without reference to the means for their realization, and so as ideals. These are the two antithetical forms of abstract reflective rationality. Practical rationality is the synthesis of these two aspects; the unification of efficient means and satisfactory ends. But we meet here the ultimate condition both of efficiency and

[1] *The Self as Agent*, p. 123.
[2] Aristotle, *Nicomachean Ethics*, Book 1, Chap. I.

satisfactoriness. The future can be determined only in one way, and therefore only through the unification of actions, as one action of many agents. If this is not achieved, then the means which is efficient in abstract theory will prove ineffective in practice; and what is ideally satisfactory will prove in reality unsatisfactory. The actions of different agents will negate one another and produce frustration. The function of religion is the representation of the community of agents, and of the ultimate conditions of action, both in respect of its means and its ends. Religion, we may say, is the knowledge of the Other as community, and is the full form of reflective rationality. It is the knowledge which must inform all action for the achievement of community, and therefore the ground of all really efficient and really satisfactory action whatever.

CHAPTER NINE

The Devices of Politics

We have been considering until now the positive aspects of the personal. Our general subject has been 'Persons in direct relation'. The justification for this lies in the general principle that the personal must be defined in its positive aspect, and its negative aspect then recognized as falling within and subordinated to the positive. In this chapter we must turn our attention to this negative aspect of the general theme, and consider persons in indirect relation. Broadly speaking, this negative aspect is economic. But it is the negative aspect of a society of persons, and is, therefore, intentional. It is an intentional co-operation in work, that is, action directed upon the world-as-means, to the corporate production and distribution of the means of personal life in society. This co-operation in work establishes a nexus of indirect relations between all the members of the co-operating group, irrespective of their personal relations, whether these are positive or negative or non-existent. Such relations are not relations of persons as persons, but only as workers; they are relations of the functions which each person performs in the co-operative association; and if this aspect of the personal is abstracted, and considered in isolation, every person is identified with his function. He *is* a miner, or a tinsmith, or a doctor, or a teacher.

Now this economic aspect of the personal—the working life— is both intentional and for the sake of the personal life. As intentional, it is not mere matter of fact. It must be produced, maintained and developed by deliberate effort. As negative—

being for the sake of the personal life to which it is the means—
it requires to be justified by reference to the personal life which
makes it possible. In itself, the economic nexus of relation is
purely pragmatic. Its standard is efficiency, and its problematic
is in terms of efficiency and inefficiency. Its aim is to deliver the
goods, in the maximum quantity, quality and variety for a
given expenditure of labour. From the economic point of view,
every person is a potential source of energy and skill to be used
with the maximum of efficiency in the mechanism of production.
He is himself a means to an end, and this end is the production
of the means of life. It is, therefore, not self-justifying; it must be
judged as a whole by the place it plays in the personal lives of all
the workers. An economic efficiency which is achieved at the
expense of the personal life is self-condemned, and in the end
self-frustrating. The mobility of labour, for example, is a good
thing from the economic point of view. It is a condition of
efficiency in the system of production. From the personal point
of view, it is an evil, though it may be justified under special
circumstances as the lesser of two evils. For the mobility of labour
means a continuous breaking of the nexus of direct relations
between persons and between a person and his natural environment; and it is on the continuity of these relations that the
development of the personal life must depend. The more mobile
the workers are, the more frequently they are cut off from their
roots, and forced to grow new ones. The end result can only be
the destruction of the family and the production of the 'mass-
man'. At the same time the economic field is, for all workers, a
field of necessity, not of freedom. The work must go on,
irrespective of the particular intentions and motives of the
workers. Every worker must perform his allotted task, whether
he wants to or not, either freely, because he likes doing it, or under
constraint, because he is afraid of the consequences if he does
not. Economic activity is in principle a routine of action which
has to be maintained; which has to be adapted to the re-
sources available, both material and technical; which has to
be made as efficient as possible; and finally, which has to be

subordinated and adjusted to the personal life of society as a whole, and to the personal lives of all its members. Necessity is for the sake of freedom: the economic is for the sake of the personal. This maintaining, improving and adjusting the indirect or economic relations of persons is the sphere of politics. Its institutional expression is the state, and its central function is the maintaining of justice.

Now justice is a moral idea. Yet when we consider its place in the system of moral ideas it exhibits a curious ambiguity. From one point of view justice is so meagre and universal a virtue that it seems hardly to be a virtue at all. It expresses the minimum of reciprocity and interest in the other in the personal relation— what can rightly be exacted from him if it is refused. We contrast it with mercy, with generosity, with benevolence, with all these moral qualities which express a positive readiness to sacrifice self-interest for the sake of others. I can demand justice for myself from others, and even enforce it, but not benevolence or generosity or affection. In such conditions justice seems essentially negative; a kind of zero or lower limit of moral behaviour. On the other hand, justice can appear as the very essence of morality without which the higher virtues lose their moral quality. To spend the money that should have paid my debts unselfishly upon those whose need touches my sympathy is positively immoral; and the mother who devotes her care and affection to one of her children at the expense of the others is a bad mother. The care for another which fails in justice loses its moral character, whatever other moral qualities it may display. From this point of view, justice seems to be the *sine qua non* of all morality, the very essence of righteousness, in a sense the whole of morality.

If we take both these aspects together, we have another example of the form of the personal. Justice is that negative aspect of morality which is necessary to the constitution of the positive, though subordinate within it. Morality can only be defined through its positive aspect, yet it can only be realized through its own negative. Without justice, morality becomes illusory and sentimental, the mere appearance of morality. The reason for this lies quite clearly in the fact that justice safeguards the inclusiveness of the moral reference, and so the unity of the Other. To be generous without being just is to be generous to some at the expense of others; and so to produce a minor mutuality which is hostile to the interests of the larger community. It is to create and defend a corporate self-interest, and this destroys the universality of the moral reference. To be more than just to some and less than just to the others is to be unjust to all.

Morality, we have seen, expresses the necessary and universal intention to maintain community, as the condition of freedom. But community can only be actual in direct personal relations, since we can only be actually in fellowship with those whom we know personally. Where relations are indirect it can only be potential; and this means that if we did come into direct relation with another person the relation would be positively motived. The full realization of the moral intention can only be reached in a relation between two persons in which each cares wholly for the other, and for himself only for the sake of the other. In such a relation, it would seem there is no place for justice. It would appear to be completely transcended by the abolition of self-interest. But this is not the case. Even in such an ideal, if it could be achieved, the negative aspect would still be present, though completely subordinated to the positive, and functioning as a differentiating force within it. In the relation of two agents, this means that each remains himself and differentiated from the other; there must be no self-identification of one with the other, or the reciprocity will be lost and the heterocentricity of the relation will be only apparent. There is, for instance, a kind of generosity which is completely self-interested. If in my relation with you I insist on behaving generously towards you and refuse to accept your generosity in return, I make myself the giver and you the recipient. This is unjust to you. I put you in my debt and refuse to let you repay the debt. In that case I make the relation an unequal one. You are to have continual cause to be grateful to me, but I am not to be grateful to you. This is the worst kind of tyranny, and is shockingly unfair to you. It destroys the mutuality of the personal by destroying the equality which is its negative aspect. To maintain equality of persons in relation is justice; and without it generosity becomes purely sentimental and wholly egocentric. My care for you is only moral if it includes the intention to preserve your freedom as an agent, which is your independence of me. Even if you wish to be dependent on me, it is my business, for your sake, to prevent it. This is the problematic of personal relations, and it is therefore a religious problematic in terms of the distinction between real and unreal. I can love another person either for his sake or for my own sake. In either case my feeling for the other is, *qua* feeling, the same. The question is whether I *really* love him or not. The verification of this problematic lies in the answer to another question. 'If my love is not reciprocated, does it turn to resentment and hatred?'

But now, if the negative aspect of morality, which is justice, is considered by itself, it appears as the minimum requirement of morality in all personal relations, whether positive or negative, direct or indirect. If we are opponents, either in play or in earnest, you and I must play fair and fight fair. This is no more than the minimum required to recognize, in the intentionality of action, that you are also a person, and that the struggle is itself, however negative, a relation of persons. But the requirement of justice in our actions has a wider sweep; it is the bond, not of community indeed—because for community much more is required—but of society; of any form of co-operation which is a co-operation of persons. Wherever there is a *de facto* relation between myself and another person; wherever my activity and his activity are functionally related in the nexus of human co-operation, I am under a moral obligation to act in a way that is just and fair to him. For my freedom of action then depends on his, and I must not exercise my freedom at the expense of his. I cannot, indeed, do so without doing him an injury.

Now in my *direct* relations with others, whether these are

personal or impersonal, I can hope to secure justice in my dealings with them by limiting my activities for the sake of their interests, provided they will do the same in their dealings with me. For I am in communication with them, and we can consult together and come to an agreement about what is fair to each of us, so far as our separate courses of action affect one another and impinge upon one another. This can be achieved by a common consent to general principles by reference to which each of us can determine what would or would not be fair to the other person if we did it. Such agreement is a contract between us, which presupposes the intention to secure justice and to act justly. It determines reciprocal rights and obligations which we engage ourselves to respect. It is a pragmatic device to secure justice in co-operation and to eliminate injustice. If we do not trust one another to keep the contract we shall need some further device to provide a pragmatic security against the danger that someone may break it. The contract will require a sanction, and this can only be someone with authority and power to enforce it.

Such a nexus of social relationship, unqualified and generalized without limit, is Hobbes's Leviathan. But clearly the qualification 'if we do not trust one another' cannot be ignored; and the generalization without limit is inadmissible. The possibility of the State depends upon an existing habit of co-operation which needs no enforcement; upon the existence of a society in which people do trust one another for the most part, though not under every condition or in all cases. The power of the State, as Hobbes himself admits, is derived from its citizens. In the end it rests upon this, that where their own interests are not involved people will see to it that the peace is kept and that injustice is not permitted. When we act unjustly we make an exception in our own favour. But we will not make the exception in favour of other people whose interests are not our own. Provided a customary social co-operation exists, provided we do in practice trust the majority of people to do in most circumstances what is expected of them, it is possible to devise mechanisms for dealing with the exceptions; to set up judges and kings and other officials; to provide them with police to take care of these things for us. Otherwise it is not possible. The power of any government rests upon the sanction of public opinion; upon the universal and necessary intention to maintain social co-operation. Once a system of government has itself become a social habit, the universal need for peaceful co-operation is so strong a sanction that misgovernment must be very flagrant and very widespread before any society will withdraw the consent to the operations in which its power consists.

This habit of co-operation in society is a presupposition of the possibility of politics; and in the end even of tyrannical politics. But this habit itself must be established and maintained. In its turn it rests upon the existence of community—in particular upon the family—as a group of people who love one another. It was in the family that society originated; and it is in the family that the habit of social co-operation is learned afresh by every new generation. Thus the state depends upon society and society depends upon community.

So long as a society is small enough for all its members to know one another, there is no need for the State, or for legislation. The custom of life is sufficient to provide the rules that are necessary, and the sanction of public opinion is enough to see that they are kept. Religion, on the one hand, and education on the other are the primary needs: the one is the business of the family, to hand on the customary way of life from one generation to the next; the other is the means of extending the spirit of the family beyond its boundaries to the society as a whole. The necessity for the State and for politics arises with the breakdown of the customary community of direct personal relations; and in our own European history we can read the story of the transition to a wider society of indirect relations in the literature of ancient Greece. Politics, in fact and in conception, emerged with the breakdown of the self-sufficiency of the city-state (as we misleadingly call it) through the introduction of coined money, a market economy and overseas trade. For this produced a nexus of economic co-operation which linked the members of these small communities with one another and with the barbarian world beyond their borders. It was this growth of a system of indirect personal relations, superimposed upon the direct relations within the separate communities, which made politics a necessity; because by making the cities economically interdependent it created a tension of interests within each city and a struggle of parties for the control of the city. Law began to differentiate itself from custom; individual interest from the interest of society. The city could only be maintained by law backed by force. How transitional the Greek experience was can be seen in this, that for Plato the problem of justice has become the inclusive problem of life, for the individual and for society alike; while for Aristotle morality has become a department of politics.

Yet though in this way economic development created politics and the germinal form of the State, it created them in a form which could not solve the problem. The nexus of indirect relationship was not coincident with the limits of political control. The Greek cities found themselves in a situation very like our own; a situation in which a multiplicity of independent and exclusive societies must each seek to control, in its own interests, and adjust to its own needs, an economic nexus of relations of which it constituted only a fragment. The whole Greek way of life was doomed; and the emergence of politics could only hasten the breakdown which it sought to prevent. A political unification of the Greek world might have saved the situation, and a movement for federal union did arise. But, like all Greek political conceptions, it was too idealistic to succeed. What was required was a pragmatic device which could keep the peace between communities which were culturally heterogeneous, and which would prove effective over the whole field of economic interdependence. The possibility was ended by the battle of Chaeronea; and the era of the small community gave place to the age of empire. But the problem of keeping the peace within a political society of heterogeneous groups in indirect and competitive relations was only solved by the Romans, and not effectively by them until Augustus Caesar imposed the Roman peace upon the Mediterranean world.

Our question, however, is not historical, but philosophical. How can justice, as a universal moral obligation upon all persons in relation, be discharged when their relations are *indirect*? The answer must lie in the invention of a mechanism which will automatically adjust the relations between the individuals concerned in such a fashion that the activities of each do not injure the others. This mechanism is the law, conceived as the Romans conceived it, as a device for keeping the peace. Since it is a means to an end, its value is pragmatic; it must be judged by reference to its efficiency. The problematic of law might be expressed by defining it as the minimum of interference with the practical freedom of the individual which is necessary to keep the peace. Too little interference, equally with too much, will make the law inefficient for its purpose; for in either case it will provide a motive for a breach of the peace. This motive is the sense of injustice; the feeling in individuals or groups that they are being unfairly restricted relative to others.

When we talk of the law, in this sense, we are not thinking merely of a set of rules or principles, but of the whole set of devices which are necessary to make the laws operative for their purpose. The law has to be determined, formulated, amended and adapted to changing circumstances. It has to be interpreted and applied to particular cases; it has to be administered and enforced. The whole apparatus for the promulgation, interpretation and administration of law is the State. The State is power in the service of law; and law is the means to justice in the indirect relations of the members of an association of persons co-operating for the production and distribution of the means of personal life.

We may now turn to consider the grounds of political obligation. The question is often put in the form, 'Why ought I to obey the law?' But in this form the question is too imprecise to be answered without qualification. For firstly, it is metaphorical. Strictly speaking, I cannot obey a law, but only a person; and in a derivative sense, a command addressed to me by a person. But I am not under an obligation to obey the commands of any legal functionary except in so far as he is acting within the authority with which the law invests him. If a policeman were to order me to hand over my watch and pocket book to him I should be under no obligation to obey him, unless he could show legal authority for the demand. We must amend the question, and ask, 'Why ought I to conform to the law?' But again, this question cannot be answered without qualification. The law does not require an unqualified conformity. Suppose that I am the eldest of three brothers, and that my father dies intestate in a society in which the law of inheritance gives me the right to be his sole heir. If I get my three brothers together and say to them, 'Let us divide our father's property into four equal parts and each take one share', I do not conform to the law, yet the law does not object. I am free to act as I please, provided all the persons affected are satisfied. It is indeed quite common for a legal officer to suggest to the parties to a legal dispute that they would be well advised to settle their dispute out of court. It is important to recognize that the law does not act automatically, but only if a complaint has been laid; even if, in certain types of case, the State makes it the duty of one of its functionaries to see that a complaint is laid. It is clear, then, that we are not under an unconditional obligation to conform our actions to the law.

We must go farther, however. If it should happen that conformity to the law would involve me in acting immorally, or even in doing something which to the best of my judgment would be immoral, I am under a moral obligation to refuse to conform to the law. Whatever obligation I may have in respect of the law, it certainly cannot take precedence of a moral obligation.

Does this mean that there are two kinds of obligation, one moral, the other political, and that political obligation is binding on me provided it is compatible with my moral obligation? Such a separation of moral and political obligation could only be maintained theoretically. It is impossible in practice to divide my activities into two kinds—those which are to be judged morally and those which are to be judged politically. Even if political obligation does not cover the whole field of my behaviour, morality certainly does. We cannot just distinguish morals and politics, and leave it at that; we must know their relation to one another, even if only to enable us to devise laws which will not come into conflict with the requirements of morality.

The proper answer, if our earlier analysis is correct, must be that political obligation is a derivative and indirect moral obligation. We have a moral obligation to be just, to act always in a manner that is fair to all those persons who are affected by our actions. In our direct dealings with other people we can discharge this obligation directly, so far as an agreement exists or can be reached between us. But where our actions affect the fortunes of people whom we do not know; where the effect of our actions upon them is unknown to us; where our practical relations are indirect, we cannot act justly on our own judgment, however much we may wish to do so. In this field the justice of our actions depends upon a system of law which automatically achieves the adjustment which we require. The moral obligation to act justly then carries with it a derivative obligation to maintain the means to justice, and this is a system of effective law. We have, therefore, a moral obligation to maintain the law as the necessary means to justice. Here, if anywhere, to will the end is to will the means to it.

This moral obligation is not discharged simply by refraining from transgressing the particular laws which are enforced by the state. There may, on occasion, be an obligation to refuse to conform to a law. In that case, however, the obligation must be to act in a way which is compatible with maintaining the system of law and which aims at its amendment, not its abrogation; in a way that makes law not less but more effective. In general, this must mean that in refusing to conform to the law I recognize the law, and the duty of the State to apply the law; and that I am prepared to accept whatever penalty the courts may decide to enforce against me. In so doing I do not recognize that the law is just, only that the law is the law, and that the law is a necessary means to justice. What I may not do is to make myself judge in my own case; and the reason for this is that justice refers to my indirect relations to other persons. The claim to be treated justly does indeed refer to my private interests, but not in themselves; rather in relation to those of all others who are affected by my actions. The claim to justice is a claim to have my interests considered equally with those of all the others, and this can only be settled by a general rule which is external to the particular claim I make. My case must be subsumed under a general principle which is the same for all like cases. This is the significance of 'equality before the law'; of the principle that each must count for one and nobody for more than one. It is the negative aspect of personal equality. Its negativity lies in this, that it concerns the relations of individuals who co-operate without being in direct personal relation to one another. The effect of the behaviour of one of us upon the others is in such cases purely *de facto*, and not matter of intention. What makes these relations personal, though indirect, is that each of us intends to maintain the system of co-operation in general. The relation between any two persons in such a system is indirectly intentional; it is a relation of their functions in the system rather than of themselves as persons.

It would not serve our formal purpose to elaborate the treatment of this issue farther, in spite of the many interesting questions which it raises. The central point is that law, and the structure of the State which law requires, is a system of devices. The State, as the legal organization of society, is essentially pragmatic: it is the technological aspect of society. Consequently, its only value lies in its efficiency: it is a means, not an end, and has no intrinsic value in itself. It is therefore a radical error to treat the law, or the State which is the creature of law, as if it were self-justifying or had any *raison d'être* other than its usefulness. The State is a public utility, and should be treated and judged as such. It is a dangerous error to personalize the State and to attribute it to characters or qualities which belong only to human beings. Above all, to feel for the State the kind of reverence, for the law the sort of respect, that is appropriate to persons, is an emotional unreason, the very essence of superstition. To worship the State is to indulge in idolatry. To personify the State is to pervert it, so that it tends to the destruction of society, not to its preservation.

I say this advisedly, weighing my words. For if I am not mistaken, we live in a society which is becoming increasingly a prey to this superstition, at a point in history where the destruction of personal values to which it must lead is likely to be swift and catastrophic. The root of the error is to be found in the illusions of the romantic movement, and it consists in assigning religious functions to the State; in looking to political organization to create community amongst men. 'Liberty, equality and fraternity' do, as we have recognized, constitute community. For this very reason they cannot be achieved by organization; yet the democratic revolutions proclaimed them as the goal of politics. To create community is to make friendship the form of all personal relations. This is a religious task, which can only be performed through the transformation of the motives of our behaviour. Rousseau proposed to 'take men as they are, and States as they ought to be', proclaiming thereby that there is no need to change men, but only to provide the political institutions which will allow their natural goodness to express itself. But the modern abolition of sin is only one form of the idealistic illusion that we can abolish facts by refusing to take account of them. Having deceived ourselves in this fashion, we can see no harm in assigning a religious function to the politician or in looking to the State for the salvation of the world. To do this is to pervert the State and to ensure failure and frustration.

Law then is a technological device, and the State is a set of technical devices for the development and maintenance of law. Now the value of any device lies wholly in its efficiency. To personalize the State, to assign it the religious function of creating community, to make it an end in itself and ascribe to it an intrinsic value, is, in fact, to value efficiency for its own sake. It is to make power the supreme good, and personal life a struggle for power. This is the height of unreason. For power is merely a general term for the means of action. To make power an end is to invert the logical relation between means and end. This is indeed possible, and in certain circumstances justifiable. For there are types of power which are general, in the sense that they can be used as a means to a number of different ends. Consequently, it is possible to intend the accumulation of power without deciding in advance what end it shall be used to secure. The accumulation of wealth, the accumulation of knowledge, the accumulation of territory and many other general means of action can be pursued for their own sake, simply by postponing the question of the use to be made of them in the long run. But if the question is not postponed but ignored, there arises a conception of power as an absolute end, and corresponding to it a way of life which consists in the exploitation of power for its own sake. The right thing to do becomes whatever the available manes makes possible.

The State is a device, we have said; but we must now add that it is a necessary device which cannot be dispensed with or exchanged for any other, so soon at least as the necessary co-operation in society requires an adjustment of indirect human relations. Both Aristotle and Rousseau recognized that the condition of the free society which was their ideal depends upon all its members being able to meet together in one assembly and so to be in direct relation with one another. A mere extension of numbers to the point where this becomes physically impossible makes law enforced by the State the only means of escaping anarchy; the only way in which the peace can be kept. This necessity for politics gives the State a special character as a device. It is a device which is necessary beyond an early stage of social development for the very possibility of civilized human existence. This invests the State with an absolute character which other devices do not possess, and which gives it a claim upon us which they cannot have. Without justice, social co-operation is impossible, without law, justice is impossible and without power law is futile and ineffective, a mere ideal. We have therefore a moral obligation to maintain the law and to secure its efficiency.

But the necessity of law, even its absolute necessity, makes no difference to its pragmatic character; it tends rather to make the misuse of law more dangerous. For if the apperception of any society becomes predominantly pragmatic; if power becomes the end rather than the means, then the power of the State becomes absolute, since it is the power which determines, through law, the exercise of all power. The will to power necessarily results in the apotheosis of the State: for it makes the State the author of society and society the creature of the State. Law becomes not the means to justice but the criterion of justice. Morality becomes the system of actions which maintain and increase the power of the State; and this the State alone can determine. Moreover, the indirect or economic relations of persons then become their defining characters; every man is a centre of power at the command of the State, and the use to which he is put is for the State to decide. If the State has no use for him then he has no value, and therefore no right to live. This is the genesis of great Leviathan, 'that mortal God', as Hobbes calls it, to which we owe our being and our defence. But we do not need to turn back to Hobbes to recognize the beast, accurate though Hobbes's description of him is. We ourselves, in our generation, have assisted at his rebirth.

Leviathan is not merely a monster, but a fabulous monster; the creature of a terrified imagination. If we track the State to its lair, what shall we find? Merely a collection of overworked and worried gentlemen, not at all unlike ourselves, doing their best to keep the machinery of government working as well as may be, and hard put to it to keep up appearances. They are, like ourselves, subject to the illusion of power. If we expect them to work miracles, we flatter them, and tempt them to think they are supermen. If we insist that it is their business to make peace on earth and hand us the millennium on a platter, what will happen? Those of them who are wise enough to know their limitations, and to be immune to the gross adulation of their fellows, will resign; and government will be carried on only by megalomaniacs, who are capable of believing themselves possessed of superhuman attributes and whose lust for power is the measure of their weakness. There is no need to wonder how it comes about that a neurotic visionary like Hitler can come to control the destinies of a great nation, nor that he uses his power in a mad fury of meaningless destruction. We know quite well that this is how fear works in human relations. We have discussed already, in considering the relation of mother and child, that interplay of love and fear that generates hatred, and finds its natural expression in destructive fury. What we forget is that the State is merely a set of devices to make law and to make it effective, and that law is a device for securing justice. Like any device it can be misused. It can be used to perpetuate or to extend injustice. The problematic of politics works in terms of the antithesis of 'just' and 'unjust'. The problem is to see that the devices of government are used only for the purpose for which they are designed.

So we are brought back to the question of justice. What *is* justice? we ask. How are we to know what is just and what is unjust in human relations? Can there be any other standard of justice than the law itself? This is a proper question indeed, yet it is not the primary question. The really important question is, 'Do we *intend* justice or not?' Justice is an aspect of morality; it is a restriction which I impose on my own power for the sake of others. To be fair in my dealings with others means that I do not exploit their weakness to my own advantage. To intend justice is to intend that my own claim shall not take precedence of the claims of others. Justice is an obligation that each of us has to other people. I cannot be just to myself except in a strained and metaphorical sense. My political obligation to maintain the law is derived from this moral obligation. It rests upon an intention to see to it that my freedom of action does not directly or indirectly injure anyone who is affected by it. Now the law is a mere device. It has neither hands nor feet. To be effective it must be operated; and the power which operates it is derived from all those against whom it operates as a restriction on their freedom. If the power of the State is not to be misused, then those whose power maintains it—that is, the society whose law it is— must intend justice. So far as a society intends justice, the law will be properly used; so far as this is not the general intention law will inevitably be misused. It will be used to maintain a special advantage—to secure a privileged position—of one person or group or nation in relation to others; and so as a device for denying justice.

The primary presupposition of law is then the will to justice in society. The second presupposition is a sense of what is just and what is unjust. This sense of justice implies an actual society in which a norm of co-operation has already been established, and which has become habitual. The fact that it works without outcry from people who feel unjustly treated is sufficient guarantee that it is felt to be generally fair and reasonably just. Thus the State presupposes society as an accepted system of co-operation which is 'the custom'. Custom, as a working system of social habits, is simply what is considered just in the indirect relations of persons. The immediate presupposition of any law is, then, custom; and from this point of view law begins as a device for fixing and formulating the custom of a society.

But on the other hand there would be no need for this device unless the custom was uncertain or under criticism. If the custom needs to be formulated and enforced it must be under practical criticism at least, in the sense that some section of the society is abandoning the established habits of social co-operation. Now habits can only be changed deliberately; and for any change in habit there must be a reason, whether good or bad. The change itself is therefore a claim that the custom is to that extent unjust. Law, then, comes into existence when justice has become problematic. There is a claim that injustice is being done. It is the business of a court of law to arbitrate this claim, and to make any necessary adjustment. The law, from this point of view, is an instrument for the modification of custom in the interest of justice.

These two aspects of the law seem to be in contradiction. How can law be at once the description of custom and a device for changing it? The answer lies in the nature of custom. Habit is only the negative aspect of action, necessary to its support. The conditions of co-operation may change, and the traditional habits may be ineffective in the new conditions. Any substantial change in the economic system is always liable to enforce a change in habits of co-operation. To maintain justice it is not enough to enforce the old habits in the new situation. The formulation of custom is therefore the necessary means to its modification; and the overriding condition of such a modification is that it must maintain effective co-operation even while modifying it. So far as a modification of law intends a modification of social behaviour it is ineffective unless the new mode of behaviour becomes habitual. The law is not a command. This is already a personification which tends to pervert the function of law. Law is, in this aspect, a device for replacing old habits by new habits, without destroying the system of social habit in the process, that is to say, the adjustment of indirect personal relations which has been already secured.

If the law is a device, if the State is a pragmatic construction, it requires justification, and it can only be justified by reference to the end for which it is constructed. It is not an end in itself, nor is it intrinsically good. It cannot rightfully claim autonomy. The question to be asked is always, 'How far does the State succeed in achieving and maintaining justice in the indirect or economic relations of men?' This question cannot be answered by the law or by its officers. The appeal must be to the sense of justice of all those affected, and the pragmatic evidence of this is a common consent; that there is absence of complaint; that the peace is kept and co-operation is maintained smoothly and without compulsion. The sense of justice in a society may, of course, be confused, insensitive and poorly developed. But it is the only pragmatic standard available. This, it may be said, cannot guarantee absolute justice. But is such a concept as 'absolute justice' ever meaningful, any more than a concept of absolute mercy would be? If all parties to a bargain are satisfied with their bargain then the arrangement is fair to them all. Justice, after all, is the negative aspect of morality only, the minimum of morality which can be demanded as necessary to the co-operation of free agents; the negative of habitual rightness in action without which all the positive aspects of morality lose their rightness.

Law may be misused, as we have seen. But it may also be inadequate as an instrument for its purpose. One aspect of this inadequacy is of special significance at the present time. The presupposition of law is an economic nexus of indirect relations which constitutes a *de facto* unity of co-operation. For this reason law will be inadequate to its purpose unless all the persons whose actions affect one another, and so may give rise to injustice, come within the scope of a single system of law. Where trade develops between independent States to a point at which their citizens become interdependent in a settled system of economic relations, there is created a society without a common law to secure justice between its members. The various independent systems of law are then incapable of securing full justice even within the territories which determine their limits. Each separate State must seek to use its power to control the whole economy of which it is only a part in the interests of its own citizens. So law is perverted into an instrument for the defence of privilege, and for the perpetuation of injustice. Unless the independent States can unite, by common consent, under one system of effective law, they must destroy one another in a struggle for power. This happened in ancient Greece; and destroyed the Greek way of life. It is happening today on a scale that involves the whole world.

The principle which governs such a situation is this. Without justice, co-operation becomes impossible. If the co-operation is compulsory it must then become a co-operation in mutual self-destruction. This is merely a restatement on a large scale of the principles of personal motivation which we discovered in the relation of mother and child. The dominance of negative motivation in the relation of persons destroys the possibility of friendship and finds its ultimate and natural expression in an effort to destroy the other. In the political field the condition of avoiding this catastrophe depends upon intending justice: and this is incompatible with the worship of the State, which is the worship of power. The symbol of this worship is the personification of the State, and for this reason it is all important that we should treat the law, and the State which is the creature of law, for no less but also for no more than it is—a necessary system of devices for achieving and maintaining justice. If we do this, we will then realize that justice itself is not enough. For justice is only the negative aspect of morality, and itself is for the sake of friendship.

CHAPTER TEN

The Personal Universe

We have reached the term of our long argument, and it remains only to look at our results as a whole and in the light of these to ask the question which is set for every Gifford Lecturer by the articles of his office. 'What contribution does this philosophical study make to the problem of the validity of religious belief? Are there, or are there not, rational grounds for a belief in God?'

It might seem proper, in such a connection, to make reference to the traditional proofs of the existence of God. But this would serve little purpose. For they belong to a mode of philosophy which we have been compelled to reject, and even in that mode they failed to stand. We began with the admission that modern philosophy from Descartes onwards has been driven by its own logic towards an atheistic conclusion.[1] If we refer to these proofs at all, it is only to underline their failure and to add a further reason for it, which has arisen from our own study. Any dualistic mode of thinking is incompatible with religion. For the root of dualism is the intentional dissociation of thought and action; while religion, when it is full-grown, demands their integration. From the point of view of any dualist thought, whether in its pragmatic or its contemplative mode, whether from an idealist or a realist attitude, religion cannot even be rightly conceived; and the traditional proofs, even if they were logically unassailable, could only conclude to some infinite or absolute being which lacks any quality deserving of reverence or wor-

[1] *The Self as Agent*, p. 19.

ship. The God of the traditional proofs is not the God of religion.

One of these proofs, the argument from design, has seemed more resistant to criticism than the others. Kant, who more than any other philosopher was responsible for unearthing the logical flaw in these arguments, gave it a qualified approval. I should not wish to rest the case for religion upon it; but it may be worth while pointing out in passing that contrary to a good deal of current belief, the progress of science has enormously strengthened the argument from design. The original argument was based upon macroscopic and superficial evidences of design in Nature; and to these could be opposed similar evidences of the absence of design. But science has silenced this opposition by revealing its superficial and merely *prima facie* character. It has revealed a microscopic orderliness of structure in Nature underlying and sustaining both what looks like order and what looks like disorder on the surface. This structured order is breathtaking in its intricacy, and seems infinite in its extent. Every increase in the adequacy of our instruments of investigation serves only to reveal a further delicacy of structure in the order of nature. But science has only revealed and desscribed this infinite orderliness with increasing adequacy. It has done nothing at all to explain it. It is a total error to think that science has provided an alternative explanation. We must conclude from this that if the argument from design in nature to the existence of God ever had any cogency—and this is indeed doubtful—the advance of science has increased its cogency a thousandfold.

If this were all, it would yield little to the point. For the existence of orderly structure, however fine, is not in itself evidence of *design*. Design implies a purposeful adaptation of means to ends. There is another aspect of the matter, however, which Kant with his usual penetration has called to our notice. It is that the order of nature is adapted to our modes of knowing and so comprehensible to us. Why should this be so? Why should the world not have been structured with infinite delicacy, but in a mode which passed our comprehension and of which we had no means even to be aware? How does it come about that at times the scientist, by purely theoretical calculation can define in advance an unknown aspect of the order of nature which is then looked for and found? And all these ways of thinking, such as mathematical calculation, have their origin, and their primary uses, in the service of our human purposes. They are devices we have elaborated as means to our ends. Is it not something of a miracle, then, that they should turn out to be means to a comprehension of the orderly structure of the world? Unless, perhaps, something like that capacity for thought which enables us to order our activities is at work in the ordering of the world? It is this, rather than the mere fact of orderliness, which is the nerve of the argument from design. It was this consideration, no doubt, that led Kant to except this argument from his condemnation of the others. Even so, and here we must follow Kant, it does not prove the existence of God, since existence cannot be proved. At the most it makes the belief in God a reasonable belief.

All these traditional proofs fall within the framework of a philosophy which starts from the 'I think' and is committed, by its starting-point, to an ineradicable dualism. The knower is then a pure subject, a mere observer, an isolated self, imprisoned in the fortress of his own ideas, and incapable of breaking out. Starting from the ideas he finds in himself he can reach out to other ideas, but he can never reach anything that exists. Existence can never be proved. But in this situation—if it were a possible situation—existence could never be *given*. To stand over against reality is to be excluded from reality. The only account that can be given of knowledge from such a standpoint is that it is the ordering of ideas in a fashion that satisfies the mind. But knowledge is not what satisfies the mind. To think this is to confuse the distinction between true and false with the distinction between satisfactory and unsatisfactory; to confuse the problematic of science with the problematic of art. Then it becomes impossible to distinguish fact from fiction, the apparent from the real, the imaginary from the existent.

For such reasons we found ourselves compelled to abandon the theoretical attitude and to start not from the 'I think', but from the 'I do'; to adopt the standpoint not of the observer but of the participant; not of the thinker but the agent. When we did this, we found that we were dealing not with the isolated self, excluded from existence, but with persons in dynamic relation, each an existing part of an existing world. From this standpoint existence—both of the knower and of the world he knows—is given, and given as a togetherness of self and other.

This new standpoint is not merely one alternative among others. It is a more inclusive standpoint. It necessarily includes the 'I think', but in a more fundamental form, as the 'I know'. For if I do something then I know that I do something. The 'I think' thus refers to a reflective activity which isolates and has its origin in the 'I know'. So thought presupposes knowledge, and knowledge presupposes action and exists only in action. The reason lies in this, that in acting I am not 'over against' an object, but in contact with the Other. In acting I meet the Other, as support and resistance to my action, and in this meeting lies my existence. Consequently, I am aware of the Other, and of myself as dependent upon and limited by the Other. This awareness is knowledge, for it is awareness of the existence of the Other and of my own existence in dynamic relation with the Other. It follows from this that there is no need to prove existence, since existence, and the knowledge of it, are given from the start. The 'I do' *is* existence and includes, as its negative aspect, the knowledge of existence; primarily and positively the existence of the Other; and negatively and derivatively, my own existence in dependence upon the Other and limited by the Other. This is the formal analysis of the structure of action; and it yields, as we have seen,[1] the form of the personal as a positive which includes, subordinates and is constituted through its own negative.

The 'I do', then, is the primary certainty, and it is the certainty of existence. But *what* the Other is and *what* I am remain

---

[1] *The Self as Agent*, pp. 98, 104 *et al.*

problematical. This problematic is primarily practical. I must act in terms of a distinction between right and wrong. This means that I must choose what to do, and in this choice there is a permanent possibility of doing the wrong thing. If I act wrongly, my freedom as an agent—my capacity to determine the future in accordance with my intention—cannot be realized and in that case what is determined through my activity is not *really* but only *apparently* determined by me.

This positive problematic of action contains, as its negative constituent, a double problematic of reflection, which is in terms of the distinction between true and false in one aspect and between satisfactory and unsatisfactory in the other. The possibility of action depends upon the knowledge which is integrated with my expenditure of energy. This knowledge has two aspects. For my action may go wrong in two ways, either in my choice of ends to be realized or in my choice of means for their realization. If I choose the wrong end I shall find, if I achieve it, that it is unsatisfactory; that it is not what I really intended, though it appeared to be. From this failure there arises the reflective problematic of valuation, which is a search for a fuller knowledge of what is intrinsically good or bad, that is, satisfactory or unsatisfactory for contemplation. This knowledge is aesthetic, and involves an activity of emotional reflection. It is knowledge of the good; and it aims at the reflective determination of a centre or focus of valuation—a *summum bonum*—in relation to which other intrinsic values may be assigned an order of priority for intention. This is, of course, a formal ideal. Any actual determination of value remains problematical; and therefore, as knowledge, hypothetical only, requiring verification and liable to revision in the light of practical experience. The systematic pursuit of this type of reflective knowledge is the function of the artist.

If, on the other hand, I choose the wrong means for the realization of my intention, I shall discover that what I have done is not what I intended, but something which I did not intend. From such failure there arises a reflective activity concerned with the knowledge of the world as the means of action; a knowledge of the causal properties of things which make them usable for this or that kind of purpose, and of the constants and types of continuance which support and, by their resistance, limit our freedom of action. Any failure in the choice of means frustrates our activity by leading to results which were not intended, and forces us into reflection. This mode of reflection is intellectual and the effort to extend and clarify our knowledge of the means of action by systematic reflection is the province of the scientist.

That my end should be good and my chosen means effective are then conditions of my freedom in action. But they are not sufficient conditions. For I am not alone in the world; there are other agents, and if they will not allow me to do what I desire to do I cannot do it. Moreover, there are few things which I can desire to do, and none that are of personal significance, which do not depend upon the active co-operation of others. We need one another to be ourselves. This complete and unlimited dependence of each of us upon the others is the central and crucial fact of personal existence. Individual independence is an illusion; and the independent individual, the isolated self, is a nonentity. In ourselves we are nothing; and when we turn our eyes inward in search of ourselves we find a vacuum. Being nothing in ourselves, we have no value in ourselves, and are of no importance whatever, wholly without meaning or significance. It is only in relation to others that we exist as persons; we are invested with significance by others who have need of us; and borrow our reality from those who care for us. We live and move and have our being not in ourselves but in one another; and what rights or powers or freedom we possess are ours by the grace and favour of our fellows. Here is the basic fact of our human condition; which all of us can know if we stop pretending, and do know in moments when the veil of self-deception is stripped from us and we are forced to look upon our own nakedness.

This mutuality provides the primary condition of our freedom. Freedom is the capacity to determine the future by action. We are agents; but this capacity to act is itself problematical. It has to be realized through the resolution of the problems it presents, and the resolution of these rests upon the development of our knowledge. The fundamental condition for the resolution of the problem of freedom is our knowledge of one another. But this knowledge is one in which the dissociation of fact and value is impossible, so that neither science nor art can extend it. For the knowledge of one another, and so of ourselves, can be realized only through a mutual self-revelation; and this is possible only when we love one another. If we fear one another we must defend and hide ourselves. Moreover, since our knowledge of one another conditions all our activities, both practical and reflective, we find here the ultimate condition of all our knowing and of all our action. This is the field of religion; and in this field the conditions of interpersonal knowledge have to be created by the overcoming of fear, and so by the transformation of motives.

But this is not a full statement of the function of religion nor of the character of religious knowledge. For we have spoken only of our personal knowledge of one another, and of the conditions of its realization, without reference to the common world in which we live. We have envisaged, as the religious ideal, the community of man; but we have forgotten Nature; and in consequence we have unwittingly created a dualism between man and the world. The community of agents now stands, in our thought, over against the natural world, excluded from it, and therefore unreal. For a community of agents, like any individual agent, must be part of the world in which it acts. Man is, therefore, a part of Nature; and we individual men and women are not merely members of the human community but elements of the natural world. We have in the end to face the question of our relation to the world. How is it to be conceived? How must we represent the world and the relation between ourselves and the world?

The classical way of dealing with this problem is to represent ourselves as consisting of an immortal soul in a mortal body. The body is material, like the world in which it moves and to which it belongs. The soul, on the contrary, is immaterial, and quite other than the world; a spiritual entity belonging to an order of being which has no counterpart in the natural world, and so to another world entirely. This is the traditional dualism which we have rejected. The reasons for this rejection have been stated at length in an earlier part of our discussion.[1] We may summarize them by saying simply that this way of representing the relation of man to the world fails to do what it sets out to do. Instead of symbolizing the relation, it denies it. To represent spirit and matter as wholly incongruous with one another is to deny the possibility of any relation between them. The relation between man and the world is merely reflected back into man himself and becomes the problem of the relation of body and mind. And that relation is unthinkable; for the manner in which mind and matter are represented is such that no relation between them can be conceived. There is no place at all for spirit in a material universe; nor for matter in a spiritual universe. This can only mean that both matter and spirit are misconceptions. The radical objection to dualism is that it denies the 'I do' and substitutes on the one hand an 'I think', and on the other, an 'it happens'. Action is the integration of knowledge and movement. Dualism denies the possibility of this integration. Consequently, any systematic effort to think out the implications of dualism must either assert that the relation of mind and matter is an insoluble mystery which, if it is accepted, must rest upon a dogmatic *Credo quia impossibile*, or it must deny either the reality of matter or the reality of mind, and have resort either to a pure materialism or a pure spiritualism. In either case, what is denied is action. For if there are only bodies, our behaviour is merely a particular set of events which happen in accordance with determinate laws. And if there are only minds, then there is only a multiplicity of systems of appearances which have no connection with one another. For we communicate

[1] *The Self as Agent*, Chap. III.

with one another only through our bodies; by acting in a material world. The community of knowledge is itself possible only through a community of action.

This dualistic representation, then, we have put completely aside, and taken our stand upon the 'I do' as the primary certainty. We know that we are agents; and any theory which explicitly or implicitly denies this is necessarily in error. We have tried to follow, step by step, the implications of this starting-point. It has led us to the community of persons in relation, realizing their unity as the condition of freedom for every agent. But this community can act only through the Other, which is both its support and its resistance; and this Other is the world of which the community of agents is only a part, in dynamic relation with the other parts. How are we to represent to ourselves this universe of existence, and our relation to it as the common world of which we form part? The answer to which we are led by the logic of this whole argument is that we must conceive it through the form of the personal, and therefore as a personal universe.

From the standpoint of the agent, which is the presupposition of our whole argument, the question whether the world is personal is the question whether God exists; or rather it is the form into which the latter question must be translated. To ask, 'Does God exist?' implies the primacy of the theoretical. For it presupposes an idea of God which arises independently of a knowledge of His existence, and enquires whether this idea refers to any existent object. The problem so formulated is insoluble, for the reason that Kant advanced, that 'existence' is not a predicate. In reflection we are in a world of ideas—of images and symbols—and there is no way out. We can move only from one idea to another idea, never to an existing entity. But in action existence is given—as an existing self in relation with an existing Other. There is then no question of proving existence, but only of determining its character. This determination is by means of ideas which refer to it. The knowledge that the Other exists together with me is certain; but so soon as I go farther, as I must, and determine, in idea, what the Other is and what I am and how we are related, knowledge becomes problematical. The general question that arises is whether my representation of what exists is adequate or inadequate. This adequacy refers to action, in which we are in existence; and the resolution of the problematic lies in the function of knowledge, that it makes possible, if it is adequate, the full realization of our capacity to act, that is, our freedom. Apart from our knowledge of existence in action, which is the mere zero of knowledge, all our reflective knowledge is hypothetical and requires to be verified in action; and in action it may prove inadequate to what is required of it. This is the case whether it be perceptual or conceptual, whether it be knowledge of fact or of value, or knowledge of the personal Other.

Consequently, the theological question is improperly represented in the form 'Does God exist?' It must be expressed in the form, 'Is what exists personal?' More adequately stated this might run, 'Is the universal Other, from which the community of persons distinguishes itself, and which is the same for all persons, a personal or an impersonal Other? More simply, if we distinguish ourselves—that is, all finite personal individuals whatever—from the world, we have to ask whether the world is personal or impersonal. We must remember, however, that this is a real question only if it has a reference to action. If it made no difference to action it would be meaningless—a merely speculative metaphysical conundrum. It would be incapable of any verification. But clearly we can live in the world in a fashion that is grounded either in a belief that the world is personal or that it is impersonal; and these two ways of life will be different. Consequently, the verification of the belief in God must lie in their difference; and in particular in the difference between the realization of freedom in the one and in the other.

The formal question, however, is in a somewhat different case. What is verified in action is necessarily a *conception* of God, which presupposes a practical belief in His reality. But if we attend merely to the logical form of any belief in the personal character of the universal Other, we can ask whether it is adequate as a form of apperception. We can consider its formal implications, contrast them with the implications of alternative forms, and refer them to our experience of practical life. For the difference between a personal conception of the world and an impersonal one is a difference of apperception, and modes of apperception may be more or less adequate. We can be more precise than this, for the adequacy of which we are speaking refers to the representation of our relation as persons to the world in which we live.

The contemporary decay of religious belief and the spread of atheism is doubtless not unconnected with the rise and steady progress of science and the technologies which are based upon it. But it has nothing to do with anything that scientists have discovered about the world. What brought religion and science into conflict, and presented them as alternative systems of belief, was the attempt of religious authorities to suppress scientific research in favour of a primitive cosmology and a Graeco-Roman philosophy. This religious stupidity compelled science to fight for its right to discover the truth against a religious obscurantism which fought to secure its own power as the arbiter of truth and of right in all fields. The inevitable result was the destruction of religious reality. A dogmatic theology, which failed to face up to its own problematic and refused to recognize the hypothetical character of all our knowledge, presented the relation of science and religion as an opposition of two incompatible systems of belief about the world, between which we must choose. Once science and religion were thus brought into conflict, the triumph of science was as certain as it was justified. The truth which gave the victory to science and which justified its triumph lay not at all in the results of scientific enquiry but in the recognition that all knowledge is problematical; that all reflective representations of the world are hypothetical and require to be verified by reference to action. Science exchanged certainty for an increasing probability in knowledge, guaranteed by practical achievement. Theology demanded certainty, and was prepared to guarantee certainty by authority. In this it revealed its own unreality. For the demand for certainty is the reflective aspect of the demand for security; and the demand for security is the expression of fear, and betrays the dominance of the negative in our motivation. As we have seen, a negatively motived religion is unreal.

This confrontation of religion and science as two incompatible conceptions of the world is an error which distorts our understanding of both. There is, however, an underlying difference of apperception. Religion apperceives the world personally; science impersonally. This implies two different conceptions of the relation between man and the world. For science this relation is an impersonal one; for religion it is personal. The scientific apperception is pragmatic. The world is material for our use, and science seeks to develop that knowledge of the world through which we can use it as the instrument of our intentions. The religious apperception is communal. The relation of man to the world is his relation to God; and we relate ourselves rightly to the world by entering into communion with God, and seeking to understand and to fulfil his intention. The conflict between religion and science is at bottom a conflict between these two apperceptions conceived as opposite and incompatible.

This incompatibility, however, is a misconception. To apperceive the world personally is to conceive it through the form of the personal, and this form is a positive which contains, subordinates and is constituted by its own negative. A personal apperception of the world, then, necessarily includes an impersonal apperception in its constitution. The impersonal apperception of science is merely a limitation of the personal apperception to its negative dimension. Formally, therefore, religion necessarily includes and is constituted by science; while science appears to be in conflict with religion only through a limitation of attention to the negative aspect of our relation to the world. It excludes from attention not merely the religious, but also the aesthetic aspect of the relation. Indeed, what is referred to as the conflict of science and religion is very often a conflict between science and art, which are constituted by opposite and compensating limitations of attention. The artistic apperception apprehends the world, not as material to be used, but as a spectacle to be enjoyed. If, for example, we base the distinction between science and religion on the distinction between reason and emotion—itself a faulty dichotomy—and consider religion to express an emotional attitude to the world, we are confusing aesthetic with religious apperception. One common way of falling into this error is to ground religion on mystical experience.

The proper way of representing the relation between religion and science, then, is to say that religion is the expression of an adequate apperception of our relation to the world, while science is the expression of a limited, partial, and therefore inadequate, apperception. This is, of course, not a criticism of science. The inadequacy is not scientific but philosophical; the limitation is that science does not seek to answer every question that can legitimately be asked, but only a certain range of questions. The limitation of attention which constitutes science is necessary to the performance of its function in the economy of personal life. It deals only with questions about matter of fact. It is only if religion and science are represented as alternative ways of apprehending the world, both of which claim to provide an adequate expression of our relation to the world, and between which we must choose, that we must say that the religious mode is comprehensive and adequate, while the scientific mode is limited and therefore inadequate.

It remains, therefore, only to exhibit the inadequacy of any impersonal conception of the world. Our long discussion has provided us with many ways of doing this, only some of which need to be considered now. First, then, let us notice that the world which has to be represented is the world in which we live and to which we belong. We are elements of the world which we represent to ourselves and which in reflection we distinguish from ourselves; and all our activities are integral with the total activity of the world. Even if one of us takes the attitude of an observer, the world which he observes includes all the rest of us, with our activities, both practical and reflective. Thus, when Wittgenstein begins the *Tractatus Logico-Philosophicus* with the statement, 'The world is everything that is the case', he is already in error. This is equivalent to asserting that the world is mere matter of fact; that nothing in the world is problematic. The world contains, no doubt, everything that is the case, but it contains also everything that appears to be the case and is not. Error, stupidity and evil; the illusions of the wishful thinker and the 'nonsense' of the metaphysician, are in the world; and any conception of the world which excludes them is an inadequate conception. It is of no avail to say that all these are only in us, and not in the world. If these are in us, we are in the world, and our stupidities and illusions play their part in determining the history of the world. Since we are as much a part of the world as the hills or the sea, and our existence is personal and problematic, it follows that the world must be such that it can produce such creatures as we are, and must contain in itself the possibility of a problematical activity like our own. Any apperception which excludes this possibility is necessarily inadequate.

Secondly, we should consider the character of the scientific conception itself. The scientific world is a physical world. It consists of events which happen in accordance with unchanging natural laws, and which constitute a continuum of happenings in space-time. All changes in this world are determinate, and are understood in terms of energy expressing itself in the displacement of mass. This world of infinitesimal particles in ceaselesss but systematic movement is clearly not the world in which we live and of which we form part. For there is no action in it, and no knowledge. Everything in it *happens*; nothing is ever *done*; and none of its constituent elements is capable of reflection. None of its atoms nor any of its complex systems of atoms can make a mistake or commit a folly. We ourselves, from the scientific point of view, are complex systems of atoms obeying without fail the laws of the transformation of energy. All our movements are events which happen, not actions for which we are responsible and which realize or fail to realize our intentions.

If we are thought as parts of the scientist's world, then we cannot make mistakes or be in error or have illusions, not even the illusion that we are free to act. We cannot, then, frame a hypothesis and make an experiment to discover whether it is true or not. In the 'scientific' world there is no place for scientists. It can include their movements, but not their action; their habits of behaviour, but not their intentions.

The natural effect of these considerations is to produce a philosophical dualism. The material world must be supplemented by a mental world to provide for subjects who know the material world, though they are not included in it. But this way out is closed to us, since it is not merely knowledge that is excluded, but action. As agents we are part of the world we know. We must conclude, therefore, that the physical world is an imaginary world, and not the world in which we exist. A world in which there are no persons is not the real world. But if the physical world is a construct of the imagination it is a valid construct, not mere phantasy. It refers, even if problematically, to the real world in one of its aspects. What excludes the personal from this imaginary world is the intention of science. The scientist—and, of course, the ordinary man when he is using things to achieve his purposes—limits his attention to the impersonal aspect of the world, and so excludes its personal aspect. On the other hand, if we apperceive the world personally, its impersonal aspect is not excluded. It is necessary to the constitution of its personal character. The religious apperception is inclusive and adequate; the scientific exclusive and inadequate.

Thirdly, the same conclusion is reached if we consider the character of our knowledge of existence. What is given immediately in action is the existence of self and other in practical relation. In action, I know that I exist as agent, and that the Other exists as resistance and support of my action. The rule governing the process through which I seek to determine the character of the Other is this; I must determine myself and the Other reciprocally, by means of the same categories. Whatever formal characters I ascribe to the Other, I must ascribe to myself, and vice versa. If I determine the Other merely as body, I must determine myself merely as body; if as a system of energy, then I must determine myself reciprocally as a system of energy. But I know that the energy I exert in action is intentionally determined, and this I express by saying that I am an agent who does things, and whose acts are not merely events which happen. Consequently, I must characterize the Other in the same terms, as an Agent acting intentionally in relation to me. If I determine myself as agent and the world as a system of energy which is impersonal, then I conclude, irrationally, that I am the only agent, and that I am not part of the world in which I act. We should recall here an earlier conclusion, that the personal conception of the world is not the result of personifying what is first recognized as non-personal. The personal conception of the Other is original; and the conception of the impersonal is reached through a process of depersonalization, and remains always more or less ambiguous.[1]

Finally, we come back to the common-sense distinction between 'what is done' and 'what simply happens', which forms the *prima facie* starting-point of any attempt to understand action. We understand what is done by reference to the intention of an agent. What merely happens we refer to another happening which we call its cause. Actions are the realization of intentions; events the effects of causes. But these two sorts of change which we distinguish are so closely intertwined in the process of the world, and so indistinguishable by observation, that it is impossible to accept the distinction as ultimate. What happens in the world determines, through our knowledge of it, the changes in our intentions; and the actions we perform have consequences which were not intended. The world is one continuum in time, and our actions as well as the events which happen are equally elements, and necessarily interrelated elements, in this single continuum. There would appear then to be only two ways in which this unity of doings and happenings can be thought. We may reduce actions to events; or we may

---

[1] *Supra*, pp. 74 f.

raise events to the level of action. We may say that either what appears to be action is really event, or that what appears to be mere happening is really action. Have we any grounds for choosing between these two alternatives?

We have the best of reasons. Only one of the alternatives is thinkable. Because the 'I do' is our primary certainty, it is impossible to think that all our actions are merely events which happen, and which must be ascribed to causes, not to intentions. To think this would be to think that the world is a complex process of events in time, which is informed by no intention and is, therefore, completely meaningless. But this process includes ourselves and all our activities, and as parts of the process they too must be meaningless and devoid of intention. This must be taken strictly: it must mean that we never act; that we cannot form an intention and seek to realize it; that nothing that we do or say or think is, or can be, meaningful. All our freedom, theoretical as well as practical, must be an illusion. In that case, we cannot know that the world is a process of events, for nothing that we say can be meaningful. And this is self-contradictory; for if it were true we could not know that it was true; indeed, we should be creatures who could not even provide an asylum for illusions.

There is, then, only one way in which we can think our relation to the world, and that is to think it as a personal relation, through the form of the personal. We must think that the world is one action, and that its impersonal aspect is the negative aspect of this unity of action, contained in it, subordinated within it, and necessary to its constitution. To conceive the world thus is to conceive it as the act of God, the Creator of the world, and ourselves as created agents, with a limited and dependent freedom to determine the future, which can be realized only on the condition that our intentions are in harmony with His intention, and which must frustrate itself if they are not.

There are two further points which I feel it necessary to make; one to prevent a possible misunderstanding of this conclusion, and the other to make the study we have undertaken formally complete. The first is that the conception of God at which we have arrived is not pantheistic. Pantheism results from the attempt to give a religious colour to an organic conception of the world. A personal conception alone is fully theistic and fully religious. For there can be no action without an agent, and an agent, whether finite or infinite, though he is immanent in existence, necessarily transcends it. For the existent is what has been determined, and the agent is the determiner. What has been determined is the past; but the agent is concerned with the future and its determination. So in action he passes beyond his existence, transcending the past which constitutes his determinate being. His reality as agent lies in his continual self-transcendence. God, therefore, as the infinite Agent is immanent in the world which is his act, but transcendent of it. The terms 'transcendent' and 'immanent' refer to the nature of persons as agents, and they are strictly correlative. Pure immanence, like pure transcendence, is meaningless. Whatever is transcendent is necessarily immanent; and immanence, in turn, implies transcendence.

It would be a mistake to suppose that this vindication of the validity of religious belief in general constitutes an argument for the truth of any system of religious belief in particular. Religious doctrines are as problematic as scientific theories and require like them a constant revision and a continual verification in action. Their verification differs in this, that it cannot be experimental, since they are not merely pragmatic; they can be verified only by persons who are prepared to commit themselves intentionally to the way of life which they prescribe.

The second point concerns the nature of philosophy itself. In our discussion of the modes of reflection, we considered history, science, art and religion. Philosophy was conspicuous by its absence. The excuse for this silence is to be found in the uncertainty, on this issue, which is characteristic of contemporary philosophy itself. For a long time now philosophers have debated the question, 'What is philosophy?' and have found

divergent and incompatible answers. But it has been characteristic of the development of the debate that the claims of philosophy have been steadily reduced until, in contemporary
positivism, it has shrunk to a mere shadow of itself. All its
positive content has been declared to be organized nonsense; all
its traditional problems are pronounced meaningless questions.
Its sole primary function is held to be the clarification of language through a formal, logical analysis. We began by noting
that modern philosophy had been driven by its own logic in the
direction of atheism. We may end by recognizing that the
nearer it draws to this conclusion the nearer it comes to its own
extinction. The opposition of science and religion has compelled
philosophy to distinguish itself more and more from religion and
to model itself upon science. Once philosophy was the handmaid
of theology; now it knocks at the door of science and asks for
employment as a general cleaner-up. But science has really no
need of such assistance. It prefers to tidy up for itself.

By shifting our standpoint from the 'I think' to the 'I do', we
have restored the reference of thought to action, and in the
result have found that we are driven to conceive a personal
universe in which God is the ultimate reality. This transformation restores its whole substance to philosophy, which again
becomes the intellectual aspect of the search for the real. The
problematic of philosophy lies then in the distinction between
'real' and 'unreal'. Now this, we have seen, is the problematic
of religious reflection; and philosophy, if it is concerned with the
intellectual aspect of this problematic, must be identical with
theology, with an undogmatic theology which, like science, has
abandoned certainty, and which has recognized that religious
doctrines, too, are all hypothetical. Philosophy, we must conclude, is theology which has abandoned dogmatism, and has
become in a new and wider sense a Natural Theology.

Index

225

INDEX

INDEX

Continuant, 39, 40
Continuity, 117, 128, 187
Continuum, 117 f., 219, 221
Contract, 191
Contradiction(s), 19, 20, 95, 102, 109 f.
   practical, 46, 74, 92
Co-operation, 125, 135, 144, 150, 156, 157, 164, 172, 176, 186, 190 ff., 202 f., 204, 211
Cosmology, 216
Cosmos, 98
Creator, 175, 222
Culture, 133, 156, 193
Custom, 202 f.
Czechs, 128

Death, 62, 165,
Demand(s), 95 f., 102, 121, 130
Democracy, 145, 152
   democratic, 136
Dependence, 42, 48, 67, 77
Depersonalization, 41, 88 ff., 221
Descartes, 17, 206
Description, 130
Determination, 110, 118, 119, 130, 166 f., 176, 182
   determined, 37, 223
Determinism, 31, 32, 39 ff.
Development, 49, 64 ff., 72 ff., 91, 94, 99, 141, 153
   personal, 43, 52 ff., 65, 86 ff., 93 ff., 101, 107 f.
   social, 156
Device(s), 153, 191, 193 f., 197 ff.
Dialectic, 140, 144
Differentiation, 80, 118
   of the Other, 75 ff.
Dimension (of action), 110, 182
Discrimination, 56 f., 65, 67, 71, 75, 78, 81, 86, 106, 108 f.
Disposition, 104 ff., 110, 170
   moral, 123
Doctrine, 174, 223
Dogma, 181, 213, 224
Drama, 89, 142 f., 181
Dualism, 19, 25, 27, 58, 83, 103, 109,

117, 123, 128, 130 f., 136, 138, 140, 172, 206, 208, 212 ff., 220
   of subject and object, 86, 117
   practical and theoretical, 32
Duty, 125, 141, 151, 156, 196

Economic(s), 42, 186 ff., 200, 203
Economy, 204, 218
Education, 44, 59, 95, 104, 192
Efficiency, 114, 125, 174, 186, 187, 197, 198 f.
   efficient, 178
Egocentric(ity), 16, 23, 24, 89, 94, 101 ff., 123, 134, 138, 170, 190
   action, 71, 89
   predicament, 21
Emotion(s), 12, 23, 68, 72, 74, 131
   emotional, 31 f., 33, 136, 154, 170, 173, 177, 198, 218
Empirical, 45, 153
Energy, 17, 83, 137, 187, 219, 221
Equality, 158, 190, 197
   equal(s), 137, 158
Error, 20, 21, 22, 38, 45, 100, 110, 130 f., 148 f., 166, 197, 214, 217, 219 f.
Evil, 20, 75, 94, 141, 175, 176, 187, 219
   problem of, 172
Evolution, 12, 45 f., 128
Existence, 16, 17, 20, 22, 24, 209, 214
   knowledge of, 17
   of God, 206 ff.
   personal, 12, 22, 62, 70, 73, 211
Expectation, 75, 87 f., 93, 95 ff.
Experience, 16, 61, 88, 93, 111, 143
   human, 61, 151
   religious, 151, 153
Experiment(al), 148, 177, 182, 223
Expression(s), 59, 170, 178 f.
Extravert, 104

Fact(s), 39, 45, 84, 92, 97, 135, 174, 208, 212
   matter of, 27, 28, 39, 42, 92 f., 100, 113, 119, 123, 127, 129, 148, 160, 173, 176, 179, 218 f.

227

INDEX

Faculty psychology, 33
Falsity, 97
Family, 78, 91, 109, 151, 153, 154 ff.,
164, 187, 192
Father, 92, 109, 155, 164, 175
Fear, 62, 70, 73, 90, 94, 98 f., 101 f.,
122, 134 ff., 151, 159, 171, 201,
212, 217
of the Other, 104, 130, 135, 149
150, 155, 161, 163, 165, 170
Feeling(s), 57, 72, 99, 150, 181, 183
-consciousness, 57
Fellowship, 103, 105, 146, 157, 160,
162 ff., 189
Fiction(s), 20, 42, 208
Forgiveness, 74, 97
Form, 64, 87, 107, 112, 124, 183
and content, 148, 154
good, 124, 144, 176
Formal, 19
Free, 30, 32, 37, 144
Freedom, 31, 32, 34, 36, 98, 118,
119, 125, 143, 151, 158 f., 161,
166, 172, 187 f., 189, 190, 202,
210 ff., 215, 222
and determinism, 41, 149
Freud, 152, 154 f.
Friendship, 151, 157, 205
Frustration, 73, 148, 166, 185, 198,
211
Fry, Roger, 183
Function, 124, 140, 141, 157, 160,
167, 170, 186, 197, 203
functional, 12, 95, 115, 157
Future, 117, 118, 166 ff., 182 ff., 210

Genetic(ally), 79, 80, 107 f., 134,
167
God, 164 f., 169, 171, 175, 179,
206 ff., 217, 222, 224
existence of, 206 f., 214 ff.,
Good, 93, 124, 141, 144, 174, 184
and bad, 96, 100, 108, 115, 182,
202, 210
and evil, 75, 94, 98
Government, 137, 139, 144, 192,
201

Greek(s), 45, 125, 133, 192 f., 204
mode of thought, 45
society, 143

Habit(ual), 44, 54 f., 57, 64, 65,
103 f., 105, 108, 124, 139 f.,
191 f., 202 f.
Happiness, 44
Hate, hatred, 33, 73 f., 97 f., 190, 201
Hebrew(s), 133, 140
culture, 123
Heterocentric(ity), 122 f., 158, 170,
189
action, 71, 176
History, 18, 46, 164, 174, 219
of philosophy, 27
social, 45, 128, 142
Hitler, 201
Hobbes, 134 ff., 145, 150, 156, 191,
200
Humanism, 140, 152
Hypothesis, 89, 94, 153, 159, 220
hypothetical, 19, 215, 216, 224

I, 23, 26, 27, 41, 60, 116, 178 f.
and you, 19, 40, 128, 170
'I do', 15, 27, 41, 42, 77, 209,
213 f., 224
'I know', 209
'I think', 15, 27, 209, 213, 224
Idea(s), 17, 21, 170, 208, 214
Ideal, 19, 21, 46, 103, 123, 141 f.,
143, 145, 159, 183 f., 199
Idealism, 83, 132, 140, 145, 152,
160, 171, 172, 193, 198, 206
Identity, 19, 23, 25, 27, 89, 107, 117,
142, 143
Illusion, 16, 93, 95, 99, 101, 105,
110, 129 f., 131 f., 135, 143,
145, 152, 154 f., 170, 175, 189,
198, 200, 211, 219 f., 222
Image(s), 16, 56, 88, 152, 179, 183,
214
imaginary, and existent, 208
world, 103, 220
Imagination, 16, 42, 56, 80, 84, 88,
95, 96 f., 102 ff., 181, 200

INDEX

Immanence, 223
Immaterial, 213
Immortality, 171, 213
Impersonal, 27, 179, 180 f., 215 f.
    other, 172
Impersonality, 28
Impulse(s), 44, 52, 70, 134, 139, 140, 142
Incarnation, 174
Independence, 66, 95, 141, 190, 211
Individual(ity), 22, 25, 83, 91, 94, 98, 107, 116, 127, 134
Individualism, 156
Individualization, 178, 183
Infant, 47, 49 ff., 57, 60 f., 67, 75 f., 81, 88
Inhibition, 68, 70, 74, 170
Injustice, 191, 201
Instinct(s), 47 f., 50, 54, 128
Integration, 129, 173 f., 175 f., 206, 213
Integrity, 172
Intellectual, 42, 173, 177, 183, 224
Intention, 16, 17, 33, 51, 54, 56, 64, 66, 68, 74, 79, 80, 92 f., 97, 102, 113, 116, 118, 119, 120, 123, 125, 128, 148, 164, 166, 172, 174, 176, 201, 210, 220
    and motive, 32 f., 51 ff., 74, 110, 187
    matter of, 27, 28, 39, 42, 92 f., 113, 119, 127, 148, 160, 163, 173, 197
    necessary, 119, 123, 128, 134, 189, 192
    theoretical, 30, 37, 148
Intentional, 36, 158, 163, 186
    action, 58, 221
Intentionality, form of, 184
Interest, 80, 81, 94, 111, 158, 161, 168, 191, 193, 197
Introspection, 39
Introvert, 104
Irrational(ly), 142, 177, 121
    irrationality, 89
Isolate(s), 38, 58

Isolation, 17, 62, 67, 89, 116, 134, 137, 142, 149, 150 f., 165, 179 f., 183, 208
'It happens', 213

Jealousy, 78 f.
Jews, 128, 153
Judgment, 59, 61, 114
Just and unjust, 201 f.
Justice, 188 ff.
Justification, 12, 29, 35, 37, 41, 187, 203

Kant, 19, 34, 112, 119, 126 f., 135, 149, 207 f., 214
Kingdom of Heaven, 175
King(s), 164, 191
Knowledge, 11, 16, 20, 64, 70, 76 f., 87, 96, 113, 124, 131, 160, 166 ff., 180 f., 208, 213 f., 219
    abstract, 28
    aesthetic, 210
    and action, 21, 68, 129, 173, 182, 209, 212, 220
    development of, 167, 212
    objective, 28, 33, 38 ff., 180
    of ends, 173
    of existence, 17, 120
    of means, 173
    of persons, 76 f., 160, 168 ff.
    personal, 28, 30, 169, 189
        and impersonal, 31, 37
    philosophical, 40
    primary, 77, 86, 110, 160
    religious, 185, 212
    scientific, 28, 30, 38, 40 ff., 169, 182

Labour, 187
Language, 12, 60, 178, 224
    philosophical, 18
    religious, 174
    technical, 18
Law(s), 125, 133, 137, 145, 151, 156, 172, 183, 192 ff.
    and form, 183
    of Nature, 134 f., 143, 184, 219
    Roman, 126, 194

INDEX

Learning, 48, 53 ff., 87, 99
Legislation, 192
Leviathan, 200
Liberty, 158
Life, another, 130
  material, 125
  of the body, 131
  of the mind, 131
  private, 142, 145
  real and unreal, 103 f.
Logic, 12, 56, 159
  dialectical, 140
Logical(ly), 20, 26, 79, 131, 134, 224
Love, 33, 73, 101, 151, 170, 190, 212
  and fear, 62, 66 ff., 73 ff., 90, 98, 161, 201
  -relationship, 48, 155

Manners, 124
Marx, 152 f.
Material, 12, 80, 82, 83, 213
Materialism, 153, 214
Mathematics, 208
Matter, 83
Meaning, 20, 51, 143, 163
Means, 82, 178, 182, 186 f., 194, 196
  and end(s), 113, 115, 134, 137 f., 158, 173, 177, 178, 184 f., 199, 200, 208, 210 f.
Mechanism, 83, 140, 194
  mechanical, 13, 115
Memory, 75, 87
Metaphysical, conundrums, 215
  fictions, 20
Mind, 15, 18, 22, 103, 124
  state of, 68
Moral, 97, 114, 115, 127, 128, 172, 178, 188, 190, 195
  code, 121
  law, 125, 134 f., 151
  problem, 122
  struggle, 91, 97 f.
Morality, 100, 106 ff., 112, 116 f., 120 ff., 176, 188 ff., 200
  communal, 122 f.
  contemplative, 123 ff.

ground of, 119
  modes of, 110 ff., 121 ff., 172
  pragmatic, 125 f.
Morals and politics, 195 ff.
Mother, 50, 60, 62, 71, 75, 78, 80, 94, 99, 100, 109, 188
  and child, 48 ff., 58, 61 f., 66, 76, 87 ff., 93 ff., 98, 103, 141 f., 154, 201, 205
  -child relation, 60, 62, 65, 73, 77, 101, 106
Motive(s), 12, 31, 33, 44, 52, 65, 68 ff., 73 ff., 95, 98, 102, 109, 131 f., 138, 156, 175
  and intention(s), 33, 51, 64, 68, 71, 102, 172, 177
  transformation of, 122, 163, 198, 212
Motivation, 51 ff., 61 ff., 64 ff., 73 ff., 78 f., 97, 105, 123, 134, 138, 170, 205
  development of, 87 ff.
  -pattern, 61, 64, 66 f., 100
  positive and negative, 69 f., 71 f., 73, 78, 87 ff., 94, 95 ff., 104, 109, 122 f., 137, 145 f., 149 f., 156 ff., 161, 163, 165, 171, 217
Movement(s), 52, 70, 213
Mutual, 63, 66, 74, 99, 101, 158, 168, 170, 204
Mutuality, 12, 69, 73, 75, 81, 91, 103, 105, 158, 169 f., 179, 189 f., 211
Mystic(al), 82, 143, 144, 218
Mysticism, 143
Mythology, 152 f.

Nature, 49, 140, 165, 207 f., 212
  human, 140
  state of, 134, 139
  -worship, 80, 165
Necessity, 20, 23, 42, 90, 94, 98, 112, 130, 141, 172, 187 f., 200
Need(s), 49, 53, 61, 62, 82, 87 f., 98, 150, 211
Negation, 28, 29, 33, 74, 80, 89, 92 f., 100, 120

INDEX

INDEX

INDEX

Reflection, 15, 16, 17, 22, 42, 83, 84, 91, 124, 156, 162, 166 ff.
emotional and intellectual, 173, 176, 180, 210 f.
Reflective, activities, 11, 12, 162 f.
aspect of action, 33, 169, 84
Relation(s), 16, 17, 89, 148, 216
impersonal, 28 ff., 33 ff., 145, 176 ff.
practical, 20, 84, 113, 148
to the Other, 24, 28, 91, 92, 94, 98, 104, 106, 108, 113, 123, 154 f., 177 f.
Religion, 151 ff., 167, 176, 178, 192, 206, 212
and action, 167 ff.
and science, 216 ff., 224
aspects of, 174 ff.
contemplative, 175
development of, 159, 175
Freudian view of, 154 f.
function of, 163 165, 185, 212
Marxist view of, 153 f.
pragmatic, 171, 175
real and unreal, 170 ff., 216 ff.
theory of, 156 f.
tribal, 159 f.
universal, 159
Religious belief, 206, 216, 223
ideal, 212
phrases, 151
toleration, 157
Representation, 16, 17, 144, 173, 179, 181, 184, 212, 215
of community, 163 f.
Resistance, 17, 79, 82, 91
Response, 52, 54, 66, 69, 73, 81, 121
Responsibility, 30, 65, 83, 91, 120, 131
Revelation, 169 f.
Right, 35, 37, 119, 132, 135, 199, 216
and good, 115
and wrong, 30, 59, 97, 112, 113, 115 ff., 125, 166, 173, 210
Rightness, 114 ff.
moral, 116, 119 ff.
Rights, 141, 191, 200, 211

Ritual, 162, 164, 174
Roman(s), 133, 193 f.
Romantic movement, 45, 140, 152, 198
Rousseau, 140 ff., 150, 152, 156, 172, 198 f.

Sanction, 192
Satisfactoriness, 174, 184 f.
Satisfactory, 183 f.
and unsatisfactory, 173, 176, 208, 210, 212
Science, 18, 28, 31, 40 ff., 83, 94, 155, 157, 207 f., 216, 218 ff., 224
and philosophy, 27 f., 132, 156, 167 f., 175, 184, 207 f., 216, 218 ff., 224
Scientific, 37, 41, 45, 83, 148, 152, 154, 168 f., 174, 177, 181, 216, 219, 223
enquiry, 27, 32, 39, 42
Self, 12, 17, 79, 80, 96, 109, 117, 158, 209
as agent, 15, 17, 24, 79, 107, 117
as body, 80
as subject, 16, 32, 117
empirical, 25, 27
spiritual and material, 123
the, 17, 18 ff., 23, 24 f., 123, 142
Self-assertion, 95, 104
Self-consciousness, 86, 95 f., 160 f.
Self-control, 125, 176
Self-deception, 105, 131, 145, 149, 172, 211
Self-defence, 89, 94, 135, 149
Self-determination, 166
Self-development, 95
Self-expression, 142
Self-frustration, 74, 97, 148 f., 187
Self-government, 143 f.
Self-identification, 143, 144, 189
Self-interest, 105, 137, 139, 141, 156, 160, 188 f.
Self-love, 94, 138
Self-negation, 16
Self-preservation, 138
Self-realization, 154, 158 f., 163, 183

233

INDEX